DISCIPLES
OF THE
STREET

DISCIPLES
OF THE
STREET

THE PROMISE OF
A HIP-HOP CHURCH

~❧~

ERIC GUTIERREZ

SEABURY BOOKS
an imprint of
Church Publishing Incorporated, New York

Library of Congress Cataloging-in-Publication Data

Gutierrez, Eric.
　　Disciples of the street : the promise of a hip-hop church / by Eric Gutierrez.
　　　　p.　cm.
　　ISBN 978-1-59627-087-9 (casebound)
　　1. Trinity Episcopal Church of Morrisania (Bronx, New York, N.Y.)
2. Hip-hop – Miscellanea. 3. Holder, Timothy. I. Title.

BX5980.B738G88 2008
283'.747275 – dc22

2007046169

Seabury Books
An imprint of Church Publishing, Incorporated
445 Fifth Avenue
New York, NY 10016
www.churchpublishing.org

5 4 3 2 1

For Manuel García Moreno,
my grandfather,
who showed me the way

CONTENTS

THE SIEGE

Saturday, March 13, 2004, 9:45 a.m.

"Get back! Get back!"

And then the gunfire. The Reverend Timothy Holder — forty-nine, barely over a year into his tenure at his Bronx church — is hustled to the safety of the stairwell while SWAT marksmen take up positions at the rectory's windows. On the fourth floor of a Forest Houses projects tower, just thirty feet away from Trinity Episcopal Church of Morrisania, Adam Perry, thirty-two, fires several rounds, the gunshots echoing into the South Bronx and the historic gothic revival church.

In Father Timothy's second floor bedroom, the marksmen quickly set up their arsenal on the prie-dieu. "You can't use that," the priest objects, rushing in. "That is where I pray!" The officers ignore him.

"Take your guns off the prie-dieu!" he shouts, hearing the panic in his own voice.

One of the marksmen looks up at the priest, rifle hoisted on his shoulder. "Father," the man barks, "how many people do you want killed today?"

Sixty-five-year-old Keith Warren, a member of Trinity's vestry who arrived early for acolyte practice, pushes his way into the crowded bedroom dragging an ironing board. "Use this," he says. A marksman transfers the loaded weapons from the

1

kneeling bench and both churchmen are herded back out of the bedroom.

For a second the priest, his bald head glistening with sweat, stands on the second floor landing. Mr. Warren is gone. Father Timothy unthinkingly steps into his library and cries. Get me out of here, he prays to God. I've done my Peace Corps. I've done my bit.

The South Bronx was suddenly all too real, and in that instant the new rector wanted none of it. What he wanted was a six-figure job in Manhattan with benefits. What he wanted was an easier job. He had done all he could. Hadn't he unlocked the church doors for anyone who wanted sanctuary when the siege began? Said a prayer of unity at the altar? Recited the Beatitudes?

Now each gunshot seemed to call him out, asking if he was for real, a genuine priest with something real to give. Or was that the best he had, some keys to big doors and pretty words? He didn't like the answer. He just kept hearing bullets, certain he had nothing to give, or at least nothing real that was needed here.

Outside, Trinity Avenue and 166th Street are blocked as more armored vehicles arrive and two hundred police officers scramble to take up positions. Helicopters buzz over the tower and church. Commands come over the radio, and the marksmen lower their weapons. There are hostages, the gunman's own father and two health care attendants, all barricaded in his wheelchair-bound grandmother's apartment.

A third marksman enters the rectory and comes running up the stairs. "Father! Father!" he shouts over the sound of the helicopter blades. Standing in his library, the priest starts. "Father, you're gonna get hurt! Get in the stairwell!"

He runs to the steps where Mr. Warren has already taken cover between the first and second floor to the sound of gunfire. Hunkered down with the priest's blind dog, Jubilee, Father Timothy and Mr. Warren don't move. There is another burst of gunfire that makes them both jump.

The priest hugs the old dog tightly, scared to the point of tears. More shots are fired in rapid succession, like a growing hailstorm. Then silence.

⤳

"Here, Father, have some rum."

Father Timothy looks over at the vestryman offering a bottle of Cavalier rum and sees his own fear etched in the older man's features. "I need to calm my nerves," Mr. Warren explains only a little defensively in the elegant, clipped cadence of the British West Indies. The priest takes the bottle and smiles but doesn't drink. Or at least not more than "a sip or two."

The gunshots have stopped for a while. The priest and the vestryman have prayed a few times — some Our Fathers and a few Hail Marys for the South Bronx — but have otherwise kept silent. After the first several hours, when it looked as if the siege could last overnight, the NYPD offered to take them out, but the priest won't leave his church and the vestryman won't leave his priest. So the two men settle in, saying to the police they will just have to bunk there on the stairs because they aren't leaving. Even though they are two strangers, really, they both feel as if they are in this together, a team. Neither man says so, but they are grateful to be together.

Mr. Warren takes another swig of the rum from his native Antigua and confesses with a chuckle that when he lived on the island he was limbo champion, able to dance only seventeen inches off the ground. Father Timothy is telling him about his childhood in the mountains of Tennessee, where the point of dancing was to actually get as high off the ground as possible, when he hears the first marksmen say into his radio, "We've got his head, I can take him out right now."

Father Timothy looks across the landing into the bedroom, and whatever comfort he had found in Mr. Warren's stories and the warm, wiry fur of Jubilee is immediately gone at the sight of the lead sharpshooter peering into the scope of his high-powered rifle, finger on the trigger.

The third marksman notices the priest and quickly shuts the bedroom door.

"Father Tim?" Mr. Warren asks uncertainly.

The priest turns to meet the old man's concerned gaze. "Our Father who art in heaven," he begins, as Mr. Warren takes up the prayer.

⌒⧚⌒

By 4:00 p.m. the only thing Father Timothy and Mr. Warren know is that the siege is not over. For most of the day they have only heard what the sharpshooters communicate through their radios to central command. Father Timothy can't make out the voices outside over the echo of choppers and megaphones bouncing off the brick towers. He flinches as several more rounds are fired. He pulls Jubilee closer to him, closes his eyes, burying them into the gray fur. And then another long silence.

For the next hour he believes the South Bronx has never been so quiet, at least not since his first visit to Trinity the previous May when he interviewed for the position. He had arrived in his customary Bermuda shorts and knee socks, a white, portly gay priest who flushed red easily and spoke loudly in a broad Tennessee mountain drawl, not exactly inconspicuous on the streets of the South Bronx. But what really silenced the church ladies on that initial four-day visit was when he walked through the towers of the neighboring projects and invited the children to Trinity for pizza that Friday night.

The congregation's response was game but uncomfortable, and the priest got the impression that the church was more separated from the neighborhood than he had first believed.

"If we open these doors, the children will overwhelm us," he had predicted. When the evening arrived, several dozen children in hoodies and oversized jeans crowded into the rectory dining room, pillaging the table. The old men and women of the vestry huddled together and looked skeptically at the hip-hop kids.

"But what are we going to do with them?" several church-women whispered.

"We're gonna pray," Father Timothy answered in his booming tenor. "And then get more pizza."

It was only years later that the priest realized that his first sermon at Trinity was not to the congregation but to the children of the PJs, as they called the projects. He opened the Episcopal Book of Common Prayer to the Song of Mary and quieted the crowd. With the Trinity old guard looking on, the priest began to lead the children in the Magnificat from the Book of Luke:

> *My soul proclaims the greatness of the Lord,*
> *my spirit rejoices in God my Savior;*
> *for he has looked with favor on his lowly servant.*
> *From this day all generations will call me blessed:*
> *the Almighty has done great things for me,*
> *and holy is his Name....*

Some of the boys knocked shoulders and shifted awkwardly, stumbling over certain syllables and unfamiliar phrases. A few members of the vestry grew tense at the first hint of disrespect but the priest kept praying, ignoring the elders' vigilance and the children's embarrassment.

> *...He has mercy on those who fear him in every*
> *generation.*
> *He has shown the strength of his arm,*
> *he has scattered the proud in their conceit....*

The room had settled now. There was only the sound of prayer and faintly, outside, the street.

> *He has cast down the mighty from their thrones,*
> *and has lifted up the lowly.*
> *He has filled the hungry with good things,*
> *and the rich he has sent away empty....*

The children were mumbling the verses, but Mr. Warren and
the other Trinity members filled in the gaps with crisp West
Indian diction.

He has come to the help of his servant Israel,
for he has remembered his promise of mercy,
The promise he made to our fathers,
to Abraham and his children for ever.

The priest raised his eyes and spread his arms to include the
children of Trinity Avenue and the people of Trinity Church
in one embrace.

Glory to the Father, and to the Son, and to the Holy
*   Spirit:*
as it was in the beginning, is now, and will be for ever.
*   Amen.*

"Amen."

Mr. Warren eyes the level of the nearly empty rum bottle
and grimaces appreciatively. Not bad. He offers the bottle to
Father Timothy with a lift of his eyebrows, and the priest waves
it off. It's been several hours now that they have been under
siege. They have not eaten all day, and the wooden steps are
uncomfortable. The sunlight has shifted in the stairwell and,
as both men again fall back into their own reveries, they hear
loud shouting and people running outside. The bedroom door
bursts open. The gunman is in custody. Over seven hours and
a hundred rounds of ammunition later, it's over.

Immediately, Father Timothy pushes past the marksmen
into the bedroom. He tells Mr. Warren that he has to go outside
to see if he can help, to let the people know there is a priest
here. Quickly, he changes into his clerical collar and hurries
into the street. Right in front of the rectory, NYPD Commissioner Raymond Kelly is already holding a press conference.
Cameras and microphones immediately surround the priest.

"God bless the NYPD and the South Bronx," he later remembers saying. "Thank you Chief Kelly. And thanks to God that no blood was shed this day."

Just as quickly, the cameras and microphones turn elsewhere, and for the first time all day he looks up and down the street. The gunman has already been whisked away, and the crowd has already scattered. No one, it seems, has need of a priest.

The sharpshooters are gone. The helicopters have flown away. Squad cars flash lights silently or sound a brief half-note of the siren as they cruise off and the armored trucks rumble away. The residents of the Forest Houses projects go about their business. Children again gather in the middle of Trinity Avenue, playing. The church doors are unlocked, but no one is going inside.

Nothing, it seems, has changed. The same saints still watch impassively from the stained-glass windows of Trinity Episcopal Church of Morrisania. The hip-hop beat of the South Bronx continues, the gunfire just part of the mix. Shaken, the priest stands in front of his empty church, not sure what to do or which prayer to say.

BOROUGH OF FIRE

When he drove the dusty silver Ford Taurus up Willis Avenue that first time, Jubilee panting in the back seat, blind but alive to the sounds and smells of the crowded sidewalks, and the chicken and rib joints, Trinity's new rector had felt confident that he would build this congregation as he had the last. He would get to know Trinity's neighborhood just as he had come to know the barrio of Grace Episcopal, his first church in Birmingham, Alabama. He would make friends and enliven the congregation, win over the church ladies, the doubters, the old guard who had worshipped with the same priest for over forty years. Isn't that why he'd been called here to this place, to this congregation founded back in 1868?

He had gone to that first fish fry convinced he was in the right place. So maybe he wouldn't lose any weight here after all, he had laughed to himself, piling more fried fish and plantains onto his plate. So much for the "Ten Dastardly Diet Don'ts" he had stuck to the refrigerator door. Eat up, eat up, the ladies had coaxed, and he did, trading Southern-fried cooking for Caribbean delicacies South Bronx style.

His first sermon seemed to go over well too. The congregation was small, but he knew that it would be. He had preached on embracing the community, opening the doors between the street and the altar. Afterward he made a special effort to greet the wife and daughter of Reverend Wendall Roberts, Trinity Church's longest serving rector.

Father Roberts had come to Trinity in 1950 from the British West Indies, his election a sure sign that Morrisania's transition from a white enclave to a predominantly Afro and Caribbean American neighborhood was effectively complete. During the Depression, Morrisania's earliest African American residents came from Harlem. Advertisements that read, "We rent to select colored families" lured those striving for higher social and economic status, including Pullman porters, post office employees, and the light-skinned. During World War II, they were joined by new arrivals from the American South and upwardly mobile immigrants from the British West Indies, including Father Roberts. The dynamic mix of people created a vital cultural scene, a hothouse of styles and sounds that earned Morrisania a reputation as the Harlem of the Bronx.

Most of the descendants of the founding congregation had moved away in the wake of World War II following friction between the white old guard and the black new guard over issues like who could use the parish hall and a failed attempt to oust Father Roberts' predecessor, who had welcomed and tried to serve the people of the black Diaspora coming to Trinity. In the end, shifting demographics resolved the tensions. By 1948, the only white faces in a confirmation class photo of over thirty people belonged to the two presiding priests.

Father Roberts served with dignity during years of cultural turmoil, civil unrest, and riot. Despite the changes in the nation and the streets just outside Trinity's heavy oak doors, Father Roberts believed in the timelessness and stability of his Episcopal liturgy. Even during the burning of the Bronx in the 1970s, when landlords torched their own buildings to collect insurance cash, reducing entire blocks to smoldering rubble, the congregation found comfort and security in the familiar rites and traditional hymns. Trinity's church guilds continued to sponsor banquets and cotillions where young women in white satin and pearls promenaded on the dance floor with formal escorts in white tie and boutonnières.

The aging priest made sure the high church traditions and aesthetics of the Anglican Communion never faltered, but when a shortage of tuxedoed young men and girls in ball gowns in the South Bronx forced the congregation to discontinue the formal cotillions sometime in the late 1980s, it was clear an era was over.

Father Roberts finally left his post in 1991, just before Bill Clinton assumed the presidency in a call for generational change, yet in many ways the church remained his. He continued to worship at Trinity with his wife, Lucille, and grown children, Paula and Peter, during eleven years of active retirement. Eleven different interim and supply priests served Trinity in the following years but always it was Father Roberts who was called on to offer prayers and remarks on special and not-so-special occasions. By the time Father Timothy celebrated his first Eucharist as rector in October 2002, Trinity had gone for over a decade without a permanent priest.

After fifty-two years presiding over its nineteenth-century Tiffany altar, living in its rectory next door and worshipping in its pews, Father Roberts had come to stand for Trinity Church of Morrisania as much as the archbishop of Canterbury himself. When he died in 2005, his legacy among the three generations he pastored was unquestioned and secure. He was buried the day after Christmas. The bishop of New York officiated with Father Timothy assisting.

Even after Father Robert's death, Father Timothy felt in many ways he was co-rector with the honored priest's memory and legacy. That's the way it always was with a beloved predecessor. No one else could be as wise, work as hard, or serve God and the vestry as well. Even priests not so beloved managed to be remembered as irreplaceable after their replacement had arrived.

But this was his parish now. The rectory was his home. In truth, the place could use some fixing up. Built in 1889 and effectively shuttered for a decade, the church didn't have a working doorbell, and the delivery guy from the café over on Prospect Avenue had to whistle at the windows whenever he delivered a mound of spaghetti and meatballs and a mealy slice of pie. At least the roof had recently been replaced, although the water damage in three rooms remained, including the tiny ground floor study barely big enough for mementos of his previous life in politics, the framed diploma from Harvard Divinity School, and pictures of parishioners from Grace and Trinity churches.

He had put out some framed photographs in the living room, including one of him and his fellow seminarians, class of 1997, taken at the start of this new life devoted to God. An old black and white shot of him as a teenage congressional page in 1971 with Senator Ted Kennedy and a more recent photo with vice president Al Gore took privilege of place on the credenza. Hundreds of books remained piled in boxes on the second floor landing, but there was no getting around it. He lived here now. This was home.

When he had first arrived, Father Roberts and his wife, Lucille, had been gracious to the new priest, and Paula, his daughter, had chatted with him warmly, telling him how she had been born in the rectory next door and spent her childhood running up and down its stairs.

Now as he climbs to his bedroom on those same stairs, exhausted, the steps creaking with each footstep, he suddenly sees the guns and hears the bullets all over again. The sound comes — fast — so fast and so loud that his whole body clenches. But the rectory is dark; the stairs are empty. The projects are quiet. There is nothing to fear outside his bedroom window, he tells himself, kneeling to pray on the bench that held the guns.

❧

Trinity Avenue and the Forest Houses city projects are part of the hip-hop holy land.

Rap star Fat Joe grew up as José Cartagena in the shadow of the projects next to Trinity Church where his mother still lives, and that summer of 2004 he would go platinum with "Lean Back," rapping:

> *Half the niggas on the block got a scar on they face,*
> *It's a cold world, and this is ice,*
> *Half a mil' for the charm, nigga this is life.*
> *Got the family in front building on Trinity Ave.*
> *10 years billed legit they still figure me bad.*

According to hip-hop pioneers like DJ Cool Clyde and rapper Kurtis Blow, hip-hop was never envisioned as a celebration of the thug life but instead "started as an expression of love, not about killing each other, the degradation of our women, or bling bling." It's been called "the CNN of the streets" by the seminal rapper Chuck D, and theologian Cornel West believes it to be "the last form of transcendence available to young black ghetto dwellers."

The origins of hip-hop are as contested as the nature of God. But those who were there at the beginning like Cool Clyde and Kurtis Blow insist that the Hip-Hop Nation was born during the burning of the Bronx in the early 1970s, those years when arsonists terrorized and flames consumed entire neighborhoods. As slumlords torched their own buildings for insurance cash, the nightly blazes left scores homeless. According to one retiree, fire department dispatchers would routinely go to work for an eight-hour shift without a single break. On the Whitestone Bridge from Queens and the Willis Avenue Bridge from Manhattan, columns of black smoke could be seen rising across the cityscape like tornadoes. By 1978 the "borough of fire" was a wasteland.

The South Bronx became known as America's slum. Newspaper editorials, Hollywood movies, best-selling books and perhaps most famously Howard Cosell during the 1977 World Series telecast, proclaimed, "The Bronx is burning."

But by then this was a fact of life for the black and Latino residents of the South Bronx and neighborhoods like Morris Heights, Tremont, Highbridge, and Morrisania. Between 1973 and 1977, thirty thousand fires were set in the South Bronx alone. Those who were once residents now were refugees, burned out of their homes, unprotected, and forgotten or ignored. They existed in the abstract. As the "underclass," the "urban poor," the "inner city" they became invisible as people.

Kurtis Blow credits the children of the South Bronx for creating a sense of unity with others who lived in and survived those years, for capturing a spirit of life that sometimes can only be born from too much destruction.

"In the beginning it was really spiritual," Blow reminisces. "It came out of a cry from an oppressed people. And it was beautiful."

Cool Clyde seconds that. "People say that hip-hop has five elements, you know?" he says. "I disagree with that. Hip-hop has six elements: DJing, MCing, breakdancing, style, graffiti, and the sixth is spirituality."

Both men maintain that hip-hop wasn't originally an expression of rage or a reflection of disastrous social conditions. Instead, it was a way to show, in Cool Clyde's words, "we were somebody. We wasn't writing graffiti on walls or breakdancing in Rosedale Park because we were trying to show that we were negative or we were trying to disgrace our areas. We was trying to show that we are someone too. We have good things about us. We used hip-hop to excel and move forward."

The children of the South Bronx — black, Latino, Jamaican — threw a party. They plugged into street lamps on destroyed city blocks to power turntables and speakers. They made art and music out of smoke, "battled" by breakdancing rather than gangbanging, and spray-painted the rubble that had been their homes. Back then, once the smoke cleared, the Hip-Hop Nation was left standing, a generation whose first language was not gospel or blues, soul or R&B. They spoke a new language, or rather, all of them. They scratched, they beatboxed, and they rapped. And their party took on a life of its own.

But in a war zone, unity, pride, and hope were soon overwhelmed by desperation, violence, and poverty. After the arson and collapse of public services following city budget cuts came the dissection and wholesale destruction of once cohesive neighborhoods. With that came the drugs and the gangs and more neglect. By 1980, the South Bronx was among the poorest congressional districts in the nation. A 2006 *New York Times* headline proclaimed the Bronx "Booming, Not Burning," but the Bronx still burns, they say, and the thug life was born in the flames.

⎯⬥⎯

If you take the number 2 train to Jackson Avenue, past brown brick towers rising above scarred sycamores and tagged walls facing off with neat playgrounds, and walk several long blocks up Prospect Avenue toward Forest Houses and Trinity Church, you can see the South Bronx's past and present. A Muslim woman in a black burka and maroon head scarf passes a teenage girl with a bare midriff and tattoos pushing a stroller outside the South Bronx Health Center for Children and Families. Across the street, construction is under way in one of the lots left vacant since the 1970s and now reclaimed for new shops and apartments.

Imposing stone sanctuaries from the Bronx's early days — St. Anthony of Padua Catholic Church, a Spanish language Seventh-Day Adventist church, St. Augustine Presbyterian — are outnumbered by makeshift storefront churches. Unity Funeral Chapels and the Herbert T. McCall Funeral Home are only a few blocks apart, acting as parentheses for resurgent or surviving shops, beauty salons advertising weaves and braids, and the Mi Gente Bakery with a three-tier wedding cake topped by a plastic African American bride and groom in the window. A little farther is the black awning of the Crystal Lounge, uneven hand-painted letters on its faded pink stucco promising cocktails inside.

When Father Roberts first arrived at Trinity, the priest and his congregation were the newcomers. The lively white middle

class community that had built the South Bronx and Trinity Church was being eclipsed. The neighborhood and church
were then becoming a center of Afro-Caribbean culture. Trinity's pews were full on Sundays, mostly with fellow Caribbean
immigrants, and the priest harnessed that energy and community pride to defeat city plans that called for the demolition of
the entire church complex.

A massive new public housing development, to be called
Forest Houses, was slated for construction on Trinity's prop-
erty and several adjacent blocks. Father Roberts, his vestry, and
the congregation worked closely with the church diocese, state
bureaucracies, and city officials to fashion a compromise that
saved the church from the wrecking ball. Using equal parts
political savvy and prayer, Father Roberts negotiated, flattered,
and exhorted everyone from the bishop to the Bronx Borough
president to the state housing commissioner to spare the home
of his growing congregation. He succeeded. The corner of Trinity Avenue and 166th Street would remain untouched, the
plans redrawn. Forest Houses, it was decided, would be built
around Trinity Church and its rectory.

Energized by the victory, the immigrant congregation now
assumed complete spiritual as well as physical stewardship of
the church they had saved. By 1953 Trinity had grown to 731
members. Special committees, guilds, and auxiliary groups
flourished, and Sundays took on an air of pageantry.

It was a committed church community that worked hard,
tithed, and stood proudly apart from the turbulence and ex-
cesses of the 1960s. They valued education and sent their
children to Morris High School, Colin Powell's alma mater
just across the street, considered among the best in all five
boroughs. As gangs and drugs and racial unrest roiled outside,
Trinity stood for what was eternal and unchanging. What they
worshipped and how they worshipped never altered.

The burning of the Bronx left Trinity a remnant of an earlier era in both the church and the city, however. The nightly
arson was over, but the neighborhood itself was ruined and

frightened. By the 1980s, parishioners had moved to safer, more prosperous neighborhoods like Castle Hill, or out of the Bronx entirely. Returning only on Sunday morning to worship, they left the South Bronx alone and the South Bronx gave the commuter congregation a wide berth, like two rivals refusing to give each other proper respect. When Father Timothy became rector, only a dozen or so longtime members attended Sunday services. Trinity Church and Trinity Avenue had gone separate ways.

Today one of the only reminders of that earlier time and those people is the 11:00 a.m. service at Trinity Church. For over thirty years now, many of the same parishioners lock their cars and climb the uneven concrete steps, most all of them old now, holding the metal pipe that serves as a handrail, the women in dresses and the men in suits, hats on the grayer heads. They are proud of their historic church, its cornerstone laid in 1874, proud of its silver and stained glass, its nineteenth-century Tiffany altar, proud of its fellowship and traditions and the faith witnessed in the gilt scripture in gothic lettering surrounding the wooden nave.

Outside, children and young men and women congregate on Trinity Avenue. Leaning against the steel fence of Forest Houses or sitting inside a Cadillac Eldorado tricked out with mag rims or standing outside the Superette bodega, they wait out Sunday morning. And after the church bell rings or the boom box is turned all the way up or the incense is burnt or an unfamiliar car squeals around the corner, the old women and men of Trinity Church and the children of Trinity Avenue will pass each other by on their way to what comes next.

⌒✖︎⌒

He was the only one in the theater at the Baychester Cinema for the last screening of the night. Only a few weeks after arriving at Trinity, the new priest settled in with a big bucket of buttered popcorn and large soda to watch *Tupac: Resurrection*. Movies were one of his great escapes, and he looked forward to relaxing in the dark. He had been working hard those first few weeks at Trinity, visiting the elderly members, leading vestry meetings, planning more outreach. Even if it had been uneventful, it required long hours, and he deserved a night off.

He had seen the huge billboard of Tupac's lean face on the corner of 155th and St. Nicholas for months now. The huge gothic lettering looked like the font of the scripture carved inside the church. This was probably the last screen the documentary was showing on in the triborough area, and he figured he should see it while he still had a chance. Besides, he should learn more about this hip-hop and this rap icon.

"I almost got up and walked out because of the foulness and nastiness," he recalled with Southern rectitude. "I thought, to heck with this. I didn't want to have to subject myself to such nastiness. He was spitting so many foul words it ruined my popcorn."

But he did not walk out. Not when Tupac spit at the police. Not when he seemed to glorify violence or the "thug life," those two words tattooed into the rapper's skin, the gothic lettering arcing like a rainbow across his stomach, making a different kind of promise.

"I didn't create thug life," a ten-foot-tall Tupac said defiantly to critics of his music. "I diagnosed it."

Images and words popped off the screen. Disturbing scenes of violence and words full of rage disconcerted the priest. The rapper on screen would not let him relax or escape. "By the time you're outta the house," the rapper was saying, "you're strapped to protect yourself."

The priest's liberalism was offended. He knew the world could be a dangerous place. This was not a lecture he needed, but when Tupac said, "We're not being taught to deal with the world as it is," he felt uneasy. The longer the priest watched, the more he worried about his own indignation, feeling vaguely that it might not be righteous at all but more like the shock of a sheltered man who had not known something obvious — something important — and was too embarrassed to admit it.

"For me thug means my pride," Tupac argued at one point. "Not bein' someone who goes against the law, not bein' someone that takes, but bein' someone who has nothin', and even though I have nothin' and there's no home for me to go to, my head is held up high, my chest is out, I walk tall, I talk loud, I'm bein' strong. . . . "

The priest wanted to argue back. He was skeptical. Even if the rapper was only documenting the thug life and not glorifying it as he claimed — "I've seen twenty years on planet earth and this is my report" — it was a big leap to make, to take this rapper at his word, especially when he was gunned down twice, the second time dying at the age of twenty-five. But the movie was almost over, and he was too stunned or too fascinated to do anything but watch and listen.

"When I am saying thug I mean not criminal, someone who beats you over the head," Tupac was saying. "I mean the underdog. . . . The person who has nothing and succeeds is a thug because he overcame all obstacles. . . . It doesn't have anything to do with the dictionary's version of thug."

The priest didn't know what to think. "So who will speak for the thugs?" he kept hearing Tupac demanding.

Several scenes and profanities later, the movie was over. The priest got up and walked quickly out of the theater. For the first time in his movie-going life, he did not finish his popcorn.

⌘

"Alleluia! Alleluia! Christ is risen!" Father Timothy cries, arms held out to heaven and the twenty or so women and handful of men scattered among the pews.

The day after the shooting is Sunday, and the priest faithfully follows the service dictated by the Book of Common Prayer. This is the season of Lent, when Christians undertake "a major cleaning" of their hearts and lives, preparing their souls for God's love. But what did God's love look like in the South Bronx? Did Trinity stand for it? If so, how? Was the baptismal registry the yardstick to measure their success, their love? What was the point of baptizing children into a church whose name they couldn't even pronounce? Episcopalians were as foreign as Thessalonians to the children of Forest Houses. To them the Wu-Tang Clan rap group had a more comprehensible creed.

"Some of us might not have been here this morning," he began his sermon. "And a lot of people from our community are not here." He remembers saying something about needing to go out, to knock on the doors of Forest Houses. He remembers not wanting to.

He moves through the Lenten service, chanting the scripture from Luke 13, where Jesus is told about some Galileans whose blood Pilate had mixed with their sacrifices. Jesus asks, "Do you think that these Galileans were worse sinners than all the others because they suffered that way? I tell you, no! But unless you repent you too will all perish."

Looking at the children assisting him at the altar, the priest wells up with emotion.

He continues chanting the scripture in his clear tenor. It is the parable of the fig tree the owner of the vineyard wants to cut down because it bears no fruit. The gardener appeals to the landowner to wait one more season to allow him to tend it and nurture it before giving up.

There is a long silence when he is finished. Later some in the congregation admit the priest's tears made them uncomfortable. Crying like that seemed like a sign of weakness. Father Roberts would not have cried.

"Are you all right?" asked Bishop Mark Sisk the evening after the standoff.

The priest sat in a kitchen chair, the telephone tight against his ear.

"Like a good Southern boy I told him, 'Just fine,'" the priest remembered more than a year after the siege. "Then I lost my manners. I said, 'Are we legitimate? Are we doing any good here?' The bishop told me, 'The love of God is legitimate.' And I told him, 'If that's what we're preaching and living, then we're legitimate, but if it's not, then we're not.'"

THE DISCIPLES

The city bus belches exhaust climbing Boston Post Road to the stop at 166th Street outside Morris High School. The driver, a slight man in his forties, welcomes a new passenger with a smile, his blue MTA uniform the only color on this gray day when the sky seems made of concrete. He cranks the enormous steering wheel, rejoining traffic. None of the passengers recognize Cool Clyde now, but he was a celebrity in the South Bronx back in the day, a true pioneer of hip-hop and the first DJ to record live scratching on vinyl. His recording at the "T" Connection Celebrity Club in 1980 even featured Grandmaster Flash on the flip side. Now he drives the number 21 bus on the streets where he used to spin.

❧

Sam Cannon, thirty-five, has lived on and off in the same Forest Houses tower since he was thirteen. His older brother, Steven, was murdered right here. On Trinity Avenue. Somebody ran up on him and shot him and killed him. That's how some people do out here sometimes. He wasn't into drugs or gangs. Just trying to live his life and the neighborhood got him. He was twenty-five when he was murdered.

Sam and his brother, they stood for themselves. Their parents taught them not to get involved with people who you know aren't right. Everybody should know that. That's the code of the streets. Everybody knows right from wrong.

21

Now in his left ear he wears a silver earring flecked with
diamond chips in honor of his brother, in honor of Steven.
There really is not a whole lot else to say. Except maybe that he
went to school with Adam and wasn't surprised when he heard
on the street that his old running buddy was the gunman who
held the projects hostage. He didn't expect it either. He didn't
know him as a violent person. "It's the projects," he says with
a shrug, readjusting his Braves cap over neat cornrows. "Good
things and bad things happen here. It's like any other address
in the ghetto. If you stay to yourself, no one really troubles
you." He has been keeping to himself pretty much all his life.
He tells his sons and daughters to do the same.

~❧~

"I was from a bad block people was scared of," explains Do-
minique Singletary, who goes by the name Glory, Son of the
Bronx. He started rapping at nine and was seventeen when he
first stepped inside of Trinity in the winter of 2004. "I was
around kids who done it all, selling drugs, stuff my parents
didn't know about. They good people but caught in the wrong
thing. A lot left school, a lot went to jail, a few got a job. A
lot did the wrong thing and only a few did the right thing and
that's the story right there."

He was becoming a rough kid, wanting to do grown people
things, staying out late, skipping school. He could have easily
joined all those who did the wrong thing. But one night when
he was thirteen, writing lyrics to some raps he was working
on, something happened. "I was in the zone writing, and it
just hit me," he says now, his baby girl, Zion, crying in the
background. "I wasn't thinking about it, it just hit me: glory. It
was powerful. Just like how God came to me, the name came
to me. I went to public school, I didn't know nothing about
prayer, I didn't even know how ignorant I was of God, but for
some reason God came to me."

~❧~

The four friends, all in their early twenties, all members of the Seventh-Day Adventist Church, had run into some difficulty, not on the streets but in their own conservative denomination, trying to express themselves to God and to express godliness to other people through hip-hop. Fortunately, they have each other for support. They could still praise God through rap and with each other. They know what they are doing is real and true even if it is hard for others to comprehend. But they want to connect with others like themselves, young Christians born into and raised by the tribe of hip-hop.

So the rapper Paradox, the singer-producer Rock, and the rap duo Eric Monk and Jahdiel Newman of the Missionary Men keep putting themselves out there, praising and performing for God wherever they can. What they are doing with hip-hop, they believe, is exactly like what the apostle Paul was doing in his epistles to the Romans, Corinthians, and Galatians. Paul tailored his writing to each culture, whether Gentile or Jew, to the environment and the issues they faced, and they tailor what they have to say to the hip-hop culture. It's how they reach the hip-hop generation they come from, to share their faith and what they believe. "It's like this is just a chapter of our Bible," explains Paradox.

One afternoon they all stopped by AJ Scratch's place not far from Trinity Church to play him some of their God-inspired tracks. The older, respected DJ walked them over to Trinity right then and there and told Father Timothy, "Check out their music."

They thought of themselves as ministers too, really.

⤫

They call him D-Cross, the Living Instrument. When he was nine or ten years old rapping, breakdancing and beatboxing on the corner, he had a lot of different names: Divine Cosmic, Pie, DC Nice. But this is the one he likes the best, not just because it stuck or because it describes his extraordinary musical skill, the ability to sound like any instrument or scratching vinyl.

He likes it because it reminds him to strive every day to be an instrument of uplift, to be an extension of God's work.

He knows he's not perfect, never has been, but hip-hop kept him focused on the positive. When he was growing up, hip-hop was New York and New York was hip-hop. It seemed as if every kid in the borough was just out there rhyming and beatboxing. That was his outlet.

Back then he knew other kids were making a lot of money selling drugs, but his music and art kept him away from the "really crazy stuff, the street drama." The older hustlers and drug dealers made sure of that. They would see him rapping in the street, or doing his art, and they knew he had something. They would tell him, "Keep doing that because if I catch you on the corner with me, we gonna have problems."

And so he has been "doing that" for years. He sleeps only three or four hours a night, but still he needs more time to write, to draw, to rap, to perform, to connect. He is a busy man. He knows he is overcommitted, and when he divides himself into too many pieces, well, he can't find words to explain what happens, so he just splays his hands out and makes the sound of shattering glass. But he is a teacher and an artist and those are good things to be.

He uses rap to teach from the Bowery and the Bronx, mostly at "special ed" high schools for students with behavioral problems. A lot of the girls have babies, and the boys have arrest records and jail time. A lot of those kids have been written off, x'd out. A banner hanging in one of his classrooms reads, "I love you. Love yourself." The eight boys in this class act sullen or asleep, maybe because there are strangers in the room, but D-Cross encourages them to read the raps they have written anyway. He's already given them the chorus, and he raps it for them: "What's your life like? And what's it gonna be?"

A large boy, a black nylon scarf tied tight on his head, raps a simple list of the things he loves: his sisters, his girlfriend, his turntable, and DJing. Another boy has a short rap. "I would have money, power, I would be king of the world."

A skinny boy balks when it's his turn.

"Wouldn't you rather hear your voice reading what you want to do with your life more than my voice?" D-Cross asks. "This is your voice."

The boy starts shyly, "This is what I want: money, peace, and happiness." He hesitates. "I hate reading!"

"You can do it."

"Uh uh," he mumbles, shaking his head.

D-Cross starts some soft percussion, saying between the beats, "We with you. You can do it. This is your rap."

The boy responds to the beat. "I want to earn your respect. To go fishing. I want to catch a girl under the sea."

D-Cross shifts his stocky frame, his long dreads spilling in front of an enormous smile.

A good teacher doesn't say, "I know everything." A good teacher is an even better student. A good teacher is constantly learning. That's what he believes. He tries to be a good teacher.

⤳

Jahneen Otis is beautiful. Everyone says so. Girl knows how to work a weave. And that voice. Girl can sing. She used to work as a vocalist at Quadrosonic, the recording studio where Tupac was shot and killed. Her vocals ended up on "lots" of early rap records and she performed live with Kool and the Gang, Grover Washington, and other bigs. She "did the Limelight thing," recorded some dance music, and performed at Studio 54. In the mid-1980s, she gets on the charts with her rap, "The Gigolette":

> *You heard about the Gigolo,*
> *He's a lover man as we all know,*
> *But you ain't heard nothing yet*
> *Till you check out the Gigolette . . .*
> *She's a money-maker,*
> *A real heartbreaker,*
> *She's smooth as she can be. . . .*

Hip-hop was hitting the mainstream, and Jahneen was becoming known as a moneymaker and a real heartbreaker. She married a successful music business executive who had his hands busy with the Wu-Tang Clan. After the wedding, she figured out he was also mixed up in drug trafficking. Maybe she figured it out before the "I do's," but she was in love. They were rich, hanging with hip-hop royalty, living in VIP rooms, and believing life was "one great party with a bunch of cocaine."

Suddenly, at the height of the party, something changed. She was tired of waking up bombed. Maybe there was such a thing as too much fun. She started wanting something different from life, something more. She began going to the occasional service at St. Mark's Church in-the-Bowery because a friend asked her and because she knew artists like W. H. Auden, Alan Ginsburg, and William Carlos Williams had prayed or appeared there. She had nothing against the high life, but she was starting to believe that any life without purpose or an outlet for helping people was just that, without purpose.

She still loved her husband, but it became clear that she could not stay in the fast life he led and live. When one of her husband's friends and associates was shot point-blank in the head by three hooded gunmen right there in his office, she was terrified. It made her wonder about who she was with and what she was doing. She wasn't a bitch or an addict or out to hurt anyone, but she could not help thinking she might end up in jail or the witness protection program or worse. Here she was, a nice Wellesley graduate with all the opportunities of an upper-middle-class life, with beauty and talent and resources, and she feared for her life.

She needed to survive. She realized her life was calling.

And then, just as she was beginning to step more fully into the St. Mark's community, she was diagnosed with Hodgkin's disease. What followed was over a decade of constant health problems. Within a few years she was bedridden. Her career was over and so was her marriage. She watched as the party went on without her.

In 1993, living on Staten Island, she was certain she was going to die alone when she had a visit. "I saw what people scoff at as angels," she confides. "This entity said, 'It's not your time. You get a second chance. You have more to do.'"

Looking at herself and her life spent grasping for money and fame, pretty things to wear and to have, she experienced an inner shift, a shedding of illusions. Those things had come and gone, so what, she wondered, was she holding on to?

"It was the opening of a door," she whispers gently in the telling. "I found the willingness to step out on faith and live life trusting in God."

She let go. She took a job making $75 a week as music director at the church. A friend had told her, "St. Mark's needs you." It was not a "nicey nice" church. It was the kind of place where you had to "dig in." She felt a connection with the drunks on the street around St. Mark's, she recognized her second chance, and "like Odysseus, just when you think you'll never get home or overcome temptations, you find that you are home, you've found your center, that *that* is what you've been looking for."

Then "The Gigolette," gets packaged with Gwen Stefani on a girl rap compilation, and suddenly her dance music is getting played in Europe again and "people talk about reviving Jahneen." Sure, she would be up for touring again, but things are so different. She is so different. She still likes to shop, drink a Hennessey now and then, talk music industry talk, but she's on a journey now and like when you're on the moving sidewalk at the airport, she can't help feeling that even when she is standing still, she keeps moving forward.

She meets someone new, someone who has also survived the fast life, and it feels as if he is holding up a mirror so she can see herself more clearly. And she starts to like what she sees. Unexpectedly, she even makes it back on the dance charts with a techno mix of "Over the Rainbow." But her focus is St. Mark's, and in 2001 she gets the idea to do a hip-hop service and brings in D-Cross and some other rappers she knows.

The congregation loves it. And at that moment, she is a minister. Not a victim, not the Gigolette, but Jahneen, singing and celebrating God and the blessing of life.

For $75 a week.

⸲⸲⸲

> *Clap your hands everybody*
> *If you got what it takes*
> *'Cause I'm Kurtis Blow and I want you to know*
> *That these are the breaks!*

Kurtis "Blow" Walker's gold record for "The Breaks" hangs in his house in California. There's another one in the hip-hop museum in Seattle, and one more hangs in his mom's living room. He was twenty years old when he first gained hip-hop fame.

Back in 1980, he was the King of Rap, the first rapper to get a major record deal, to earn a million dollars and a certified gold record. He did a Sprite commercial, toured Europe, and influenced the next generation of hip-hop stars who crossed over into world culture and a multibillion dollar industry. The first years traveling were "glorious." The crowds grew, but it wasn't too long before the young star discovered you have no friends on top. He grew frustrated and started to feel like he was just a commodity. He had fame and money, but to keep both, he had to "step on people, lie, steal, and backbite."

"The King of Rap has to have his diamonds and pearls," he remembers with a bitter smile. "The king needs his bling."

> *If your woman steps out with another man*
> *(That's the breaks that's the breaks)*
> *And she runs off with him to Japan . . .*
>
> *. . . And you borrowed money from the mob*
> *And yesterday you lost your job*
> *Well, these are the breaks*
> *Break it up, break it up, break it up!*

He lived the life, but by the late 1980s the life was living him. The records stopped selling, and rappers who had tried to follow in his footsteps stepped out in new directions. Joseph Simmons, who had started out calling himself "The Son of Kurtis Blow," became better known as Run of Run-DMC. In 1988 Kurtis Blow released "Back by Popular Demand," and the critics were vicious in pointing out the inaccuracy of the title. And like that, he was old school.

> *Breaks on a stage, breaks on a screen*
> *Breaks to make your wallet lean*
> *Breaks run cold and breaks run hot*
> *Some folks got 'em and some have not*
> *But these are the breaks*
> *Break it up, break it up, break it up!*
> *Break down!*

The pioneer who had started his career believing rap was about hope, love, and feeling good, about throwing a party in the rubble and blood of ghetto life, heard in the new sound of rap a message he didn't recognize. Rather than challenging and triumphing over violence and finding self-worth in overcoming bad breaks, the new sound celebrated the gangster life and getting over on anyone who got in the way. Blow produced with some success, still toured, but no one seemed to be listening to what he had to say anymore. Perhaps not even himself.

In Los Angeles he started hanging out with the comedian Redd Foxx and musicians Ike Turner and Sly Stone. Their crew became notorious. "When we walked into a club, everyone would leave," he recalls of those years. "Anger was one of my fortes. They used to call me Idi Amin."

He was partying hard. He spent more, made less. He started using more. Coke, speed, you name it, he tried it, everything but heroin. In the fall of 1992, he found himself alone in a room in L.A. There were still gold chains around his neck and a white Mercedes parked on the street outside, but he had lost it all, those parts of hip-hop and his very self that mattered. Kurtis Blow, the King of Rap, had lost the hope and the love.

It had been a long time since he had listened to God. When he was five years old, he had lain in his bed in Harlem, scared, listening to sirens from police cars or fire trucks or ambulances. He couldn't tell the difference between them then. He could now. Back then he didn't know what he was doing when he asked God to keep him safe. But he did now.

Back then God spoke to him. People thought he was crazy when he told them God had found him in his bed in Harlem and said, "Son, you're mine and I will protect you."

A few weeks later when he found a gun, he thought it had come from the Almighty. "We all wanted guns in 1964 in Harlem," he remembers. He put it in his pocket and didn't tell anyone until the day he showed it to his favorite auntie. Inexplicably, she put the little boy in a headlock, put the gun to his head and pulled the trigger twice. Nothing happened. His uncle, grabbing the gun, shouted, "What are you doing?" Two bullets fell out of the chamber.

"That day God saved my life."

But that was back then when he was five. On this night in Los Angeles, twenty-eight years later, the sirens were back. That first covenant was so long ago and so much had happened and gone wrong since. He had forgotten what he had found as a child. In its place he had acquired another kind of knowledge.

People die all the time, but growing up in Harlem in the '60s and '70s he had seen it happen. He had watched his brother murder someone. He saw another man beaten and set on fire. There were times when he could have killed people — *should* have killed them. The only explanation he has for why he did not is that somewhere inside his heart or mind, someplace only partly recognized, he stayed true to the covenant God made with him when he was five.

After his brother was arrested in the gang wars of 1976–77, he had a decision to make. He had been a hustler from the time he was a boy, running numbers, gambling, hanging out in after-hours joints, selling drugs. He was born for the life of the streets. But back then he chose hip-hop.

Now with the hot Santa Ana winds blowing through this other city, he had another choice to make. He had done "all these bad things known to man." Now he had to see what it would be like to "live life as a traitor to Satan's camp."

Again, he asked God into his life and to protect him. He renewed his covenant.

They say the apostles were a pain in the ass, always arguing, thinking they weren't getting proper respect, getting the Sabbath all wrong. Crude men, blunt talking and unlearned, they offended the pious and probably smelled bad too. They had police records. They hung out with thugs — hell, they were thugs, at least in the eyes of the law-abiding Pharisees and law-making Roman state. What could they possibly have to say that anyone respectable needed to hear?

"Disciples weren't pure, but they were tryin' to be," the rapper Nas has been quoted as saying. "Disciples were savages on the low."

In the holy land of hip-hop, Cool Clyde, Sam, Glory, the Missionary Men, Paradox, Rock, D-Cross, Jahneen, and Kurtis were about to make trouble. They were about to bring God to the party, about to throw a party in the temple. In the rubble of the church and street, they were about to plug the altar and the turntable together and help to change both forever.

PAYBACK BLOOD

"Yo, my nigga," one of three boys shouts to another in the middle of the packed number 4 train heading to 167th Street in the South Bronx. "Biggie couldn't get no bitches he so fat till Pac bought some for him."

"Yo, my nigga," the smaller boy shouts back, "Least Biggie didn't rape no bitches. What kinda nigga rape a bitch?"

A third boy standing with them covers his mouth in mock shock, guffawing. The debate is on.

"Tupac never raped no bitch," the first boy replies, his voice raised three octaves in outrage. "She just wanted money."

The smaller boy lowers his head smirking and waves his hand in front of him as if he just heard something ridiculous.

"I serious, nigga," the first boy insists. "Tupac a real nigga. Shot five times and come back for more. How many time Biggie get shot?" He raises a single eloquent finger. "And that's it." Now it's his turn to smirk and wave dismissively.

The train brakes squeal into the 167th Street station, and it takes a moment for the smaller boy to think of a comeback. But then he puffs up, cocky beyond his years. "Biggie never run like Tupac."

The three friends push their way to the doors, the argument continuing down the platform. "At Biggie's autopsy they find gallons of grease and chicken bones inside. . . . "

Since the shooting, the priest has been walking his parish. The tulips in front of the church are in full bloom now, but the sky is still gunmetal gray. A chill wind gusts across the asphalt playground a block away where three boys bat a ball against a fading mural of a young man in windshield-sized sunglasses, the words "In Memory of Tony" emblazoned above the aerosol likeness.

He crosses the street where the words "Payback Blood" are spray painted on one of the Forest Houses towers. He takes a deep breath. So this is his parish then. His parish.

The word conjures images of a country village with smiling shopkeepers and grandmothers waving from their gardens. He almost laughs out loud. *The Bells of St. Mary's* it ain't. The row houses on Trinity Avenue have no front gardens, just strips of concrete where garbage cans are chained together. So he walks now, past the murals commemorating violent deaths, past the bodegas and the gang graffiti, past the chicken joints and the laundromat on Boslin Road with the hand-drawn sign in the window: "No drying here if you didn't wash here."

He greets everyone he sees, old men in old suits; harried mothers dragging plastic sacks of groceries and young children; boys shooting hoops on the projects courts; teenage girls with tight jeans, short puffy jackets, and bare midriffs despite the chill in the spring air. Some ignore him or give a quick glance of acknowledgment. Others nod gravely, out of dignity or suspicion. Then there are those who smile and wave, or let themselves be pulled into conversation. At the very least, his collar — or maybe it is the color of his skin or his age or his deep Southern accent — earns him some extra courtesy, but also a certain reserve. He notices how the laughter and local gossip stop when he enters the bodega across the street, resuming only after he orders and pays for his regular coffee and sweet roll and is on his way out the door. For the most part, the residents of Forest Houses respect the longstanding agreement that the church and the projects are invisible to each other.

He's been trying to see, to look closely at not just his church but his " 'hood." In his mind the word still has quotation marks around it. It feels foreign, like when he made his first attempts at Spanish with his Guatemalan parishioners back at Grace Episcopal in Alabama. Hadn't he been a little embarrassed then too by his pale skin and gringo accent? Perhaps they laughed at him at first, the burley *guero* with the booming voice and pink cheeks mangling Spanish, but ultimately he didn't care, and then they didn't either.

That's what he needed now if he was going to bring the street and the altar together. He needed to not care who laughed or thought him foolish or wanted him to go away. That's what he needed to walk his parish.

Now on Sundays, celebrating the Eucharist in his clear high tenor voice, twenty or so elderly worshippers standing to recite from the Book of Common Prayer, the priest can't help hearing the boom boxes outside blaring a different kind of litany. And when the service is over, he stands outside and watches members of the congregation climb into their cars to drive back to their own neighborhoods. No one, he sees, comes from Forest Houses.

⟵∽⟶

Paula drives the forty-five minutes from her home in Brooklyn every Sunday. Trinity Episcopal Church of Morrisania has been her home, both literally and spiritually, since she was born in 1952, and while she hasn't lived there since she married at twenty, it remains the place where she feels closest to God. She is confident in her faith and loves the rituals of her Father in heaven and her father from Jamaica. In the music and majesty of the litany, worshipping within the embrace of the saints rendered in colored glass and painted stone, she knows herself to be at the heart of her church family and their sacred services.

Climbing the steps, entering into the warm wooden sanctuary, approaching the altar to accept the body and blood are in every sense a homecoming. She counts on Trinity to remain Trinity just like an adult child somehow expects to find the home where she was raised to stay unchanged, full of a familiar and comforting sameness, no matter how many years have passed.

She arrives early, parks her sedan, and greets Father Timothy with a smile. She is happy to see the priest is wearing the colorful stole of royal kinte-cloth from Ghana she gave to him as a gift before he presided over his first service as Trinity's rector.

She wants to make him feel welcomed in her home.

~~~

The television in the second floor library takes a while to warm up. The room smells musty, like a used book store, more than three thousand books — classics, bestsellers, biographies — stacked in towers along the walls, sidling up to the old sofa and green Naugahyde reading chair. In the bookcases gilt roman numerals on the spines of worn leather-bound concordances and collected works of theologians and saints tick off centuries. The room is cool, but the ceiling fan is on.

The picture emerges on the old set and Roma Torre from NY1 comes into focus, telling him something, but he can't concentrate on what. He channel surfs all the stations twice then goes back to channel 53 and an MTV hip-hop show. The picture is terrible and even though the lyrics drop out at the profanity, the rap stuttering like musical Morse code, he can hear every rhyme of the chorus:

> *You can find me in the club, bottle full of Bud*
> *Mama, I got that X, if you into takin' drugs*
> *I'm into having sex, I ain't into making love*
> *So come give me a hug if you into getting rubbed*

The priest was impressed. Drugs, meaningless sex, and misogyny all in the first verse. Quite a trifecta, he thought.

And this 50 Cent was the biggest thing in rap right now, a hero from Jamaica, Queens. This was what success looked like in the PJs. No wonder. Video after video glorified money, violence, and women as interchangeable sex toys. He turned off the TV.

So this is what he was up against.

~⊘~

Paula used to jump double-dutch in the churchyard with other girls from Trinity's congregation. They never played in the street. Ever. It was too dangerous. Her friends in the neighborhood all came from the church. If children from the neighborhood wanted to play, they would have to climb the steps, ring the rectory bell, and ask for her mother's permission to enter inside the wrought iron fence. Hardly any ever did.

Everything that happened to her in the South Bronx happened at Trinity. There was Girl Scouts and junior choir and whatever activities any number of church guilds and auxiliaries organized on Saturdays. She didn't even go to school in the area after that first year. Instead, her parents sent her to Ethical Culture School on 63rd and Central Park West, an exclusive private school where she and her brother were the only two black students from the first through sixth grades. Her classmates were all rich. After milk and cookies with school friends on Fifth Avenue, carrying her books past uniformed doormen, she would really feel the difference going home to Trinity Avenue and seeing the drug addicts doing deals on the stoops.

"We lived between two different worlds," she explains. "When you lived in such a white world for eight hours of the day and came back here and saw the poverty, there was a lot of reconciling that had to be done to really understand, you know, where do I belong?"

Even as a little girl, Paula felt the disconnection. "I remember going to my classmates' homes and just comparing them to our home and feeling very inferior," she says. "The school sent me to the school psychiatrist because they felt something was wrong with me. I wasn't totally integrating with the other kids. But how could I? I didn't have anything in common with them."

Things were little better back at home. And make no mistake, Trinity and the South Bronx were home. At least here people looked like her. They were not rich. They did not make her feel less than. But walking past the drugs and stark poverty, she felt just as detached as she did lugging her book bag down Fifth Avenue. She saw it all, the big changes, the social upheaval and decay, but her parents worked hard to show her and her brother a different way, to keep them safe, to raise them in the values of the church, the values of Trinity.

"We were detached from it because we weren't living it," she says now. "We were exposed to a more affluent way of living, even though we had to come back here. But we didn't associate with that. It was like those people, they're not like us."

She had nothing in common with her private school classmates in Manhattan, and at home she was raised to not be like the children living in the PJs towering over her church-yard world. And yet she also belonged to both worlds, skipping double-dutch beside Forest Houses while dreaming about her first cotillion as a debutante. Even then she knew she was meant to achieve more, strive harder, make a difference. Her parents were raising her to lead.

At the High School of Music and Art, she belonged to civil rights groups like the Student Nonviolent Coordinating Committee (SNCC) and the National Association for the Advancement of Colored People. It was the era of black power, and she got involved in marches and was with the students when they took over the administration building and shut down the school. She was antiwar and for freedom — for black power.

The poverty programs of Lyndon Johnson's Great Society seemed to have bypassed the South Bronx. Things were getting worse. People were angry. Her world had grown beyond the churchyard and she was caught up in the times, exploring new identities, trying to figure out where she belonged in all that was happening around her. It was exciting, all the marches and walkouts from school, not to mention her debutante ball.

In 1968, following the Summer of Love, the year Martin Luther King Jr. and Bobby Kennedy were both shot, Paula made her debut in a white beaded gown and satin opera gloves at the Concourse Plaza Hotel at 161st Street "when the Concourse was *the* Concourse."

"It was the place to be," she says, eyes shining as if reflecting candlelight.

Sitting in his chair in the rectory library, the priest is surrounded by issues of *Vibe, The Source,* and other hip-hop magazines piled on the floor. Tupac's "Dear Momma" blasts from a modest boom box nearby and over $400 worth of rap CDs are scattered around it. It's been several weeks since the shooting. He is trying to learn. He is listening.

Wearing his collar, surrounded by the trappings of the church, he cannot help thinking about the dead rapper in the empty theater and the challenge he took from him: "Who will speak for the thugs?"

Now, with the air still sweet with incense from the 11:00 a.m. service, he remembers the angles and planes of Tupac's face, so serene despite the facts of his life and death, and his defense of the gangsters and thugs — not of their crimes or creed but of their humanity — replays in his head. It reminds him that the origin of Jesus' ministry was among the least of society, the poor, the sick, the outcasts. Jesus spoke in parables the people would understand. He wanted to be understood.

The priest has been reading Tupac's poetry, and he is making connections. He has begun to secretly think of the rapper as the prophet Tupac, carrying a message that is hard but necessary to hear. In answering the question of who will speak for the thugs, he can't help feeling that he will find the answer to his own question, the one he asked Bishop Sisk the morning after the shooting: Was he doing any good here in the South Bronx? Was his ministry legitimate?

Like many people, he had a hard time at first thinking about hip-hop as anything but violent, disrespectful of women, and glorifying the thug life of easy sex, fast money, and cheapened life. But he was trying to listen for what whole generations seemed to be hearing and finding in hip-hop legends like Tupac, Biggie Smalls, and N.W.A. and in more recent stars 50 Cent and T.I. Why was their gospel of "gats, bling, and booty" so much more compelling? Or was it just that no one was offering another gospel, or at least not one that had any meaning to their lives, the lives Tupac likened to war?

Especially now, after the shooting, he keeps remembering the movie and Tupac insisting that "thug does not mean criminal . . . but bein' someone who has nothin', and even though I have nothin' and there's no home for me to go to, my head is held up high, my chest is out, I walk tall, I talk loud, I'm bein' strong."

Yet too often the Hip-Hop Nation forgets this prophetic definition where "thug means my pride." Instead, it seems as if rap often cares less about telling it like it is and is more interested in glorifying the gangsta ethos of raw power, money, and sex. As he read in *The Source*, "At its best, hip-hop is an unmatched vehicle for influence and change. At its worst, the culture can mire an entire generation in commercialism and misogyny."

No, he thinks, if hip-hop is to have any place at all in the outreach of Trinity Church to Trinity Avenue, it will be to reclaim it's roots in respect, peace, and unity and to call out the Hip-Hop Nation's worship of violence, misogyny, and materialism.

Like Tupac and Kanye West, rappers who document thug life in order to transcend it, the church gets its power from keeping it real. If hip-hop has something to teach the church

about faith *reflecting* reality, than the church has something
to teach hip-hop about how faith can *remake* reality.

⌒≋⌒

She doesn't remember seeing the flames, just the results. She
does remember hearing the sirens. So many sirens. By then
she was living with her husband north of Yankee Stadium and
the epicenter of the fires. She was in graduate school at New
York University, getting a degree in social work.

Even so, she could understand the burning of the Bronx,
understand that kind of anger. She absolutely could. She was
angry too. As a little girl seeing how her school friends lived in
Manhattan, she had been angry because she could not have
what they had. She had waged her "own little war" at the
Ethical Culture School and they made her see a school psychiatrist for it. Having experienced firsthand the difference between
how people lived in Forest Houses and on Fifth Avenue, she
knew "there was something real wrong with that. Something
real, real wrong."

In 1979 she left the Bronx for good and moved to Brooklyn.
She's the director of social work now at New York Presbyterian,
the same hospital where she was born. It was Columbia Presbyterian then. She spent her first hours on earth in the same
place where she routinely logs twelve-hour days, sometimes
six days a week. She is at her desk by 7:00 a.m. She leads 130
people. She strives hard. She makes a difference.

On Sundays she returns to Trinity.

⌒≋⌒

Whether sitting upstairs in his green Naugahyde chair watching rap TV, attending a church potluck, visiting his elderly
parishioners, or even presiding over the Eucharist — especially
presiding over the Eucharist — the priest can't help thinking
about the dead rapper's challenge. It is, he cannot help believing, a challenge to the church. Worse. It is a challenge to him
personally as a priest and as a Christian.

Looking outside the walls of Trinity and into the South Bronx, he knew these kids needed help surviving. He did not want to accept it, but hip-hop helped them more than his church. At least gangsta rap was instructive, as one young man put it. To finally admit that to himself felt like an integrity check. To be relevant he had to be honest and "keep it real" as he kept hearing on BET.

The last few weeks he had been talking to people about doing some kind of hip-hop event for the children, something that speaks directly to them. He had been meeting with several people from the neighborhood and clergy from other denominations as well as nearby storefront churches. "I am hip-hop!" announced State Assemblyman Ruben Diaz Jr., when the priest met with the thirty-three-year-old community leader in his offices just off Westchester Avenue. "This suit, this tie, this is all really a costume, Father Tim. Hip-hop is our culture. It is who we are."

Diaz, who some called the Assemblyman from Hip-Hop, grew up in the neighborhood. He introduced the priest to Cool Clyde, and the DJ pioneer knew everybody. That spring, an unofficial band of local residents and ecumenical religious leaders met weekly, gathering ideas for music, meeting local talent, adapting the liturgy. Soon the priest realized they had a real event on their hands. Diaz helped come up with the idea to honor the founding fathers and mothers of hip-hop, and Cool Clyde, one of the fathers himself, signed on to wrangle others.

When the priest insisted on including the women of early hip-hop, Cool Clyde was skeptical. "Aw, Father Tim," he said, "you ain't gonna find anyone like that." In the end Jahneen Otis was invited to represent other female hip-hop pioneers such as graffiti artist PINK and rappers Queen Lisa Lee and Sha-Rock. But the DJ's comment and the invisibility of women overall made the priest think this is likely how the gospels were written. Women were there, they did notable things, but were somehow ignored or edited out or forgotten in the remix.

The priest got the impression some of the founding fathers of hip-hop were none too happy to learn there were mothers too, but enthusiasm for the event grew in the neighborhood. When the priest floated the idea with the vestry, Mr. Warren and Paula helped him carry the day.

Now that it was almost summer, the event could be outside. It would have to be since the kids from the PJs did not seem too eager to step inside of Trinity. Early in his tenure a little boy from the neighborhood had asked him if the church was haunted since so many coffins kept coming out, and some days he too felt as if Trinity was quite literally dying off. No, whatever they did would have to be out on the street where the neighborhood was.

❦

The women get together when they can. They used to skip rope and play together as little girls in the churchyard, and they often reminisce about what they did and the times they had during those years. They have all said of Trinity at one time or another over coffee or cake, "That was the best it's ever been."

"I guess everybody says that, you know, about when they were younger," Paula says, suddenly not wanting to romanticize the past.

Trinity was no longer her entire world, but she remembers it as the best part. She made her choice. As a child she had wanted to fit in with the rich kids at school and with the neighborhood kids she saw playing on Trinity Avenue outside the fence. She had wanted to be accepted by them all. But she could not do both. In the end, she could do neither.

Back then she had asked herself, where do I belong? Where do I live?

"Do I belong in this hip-hop culture or do I belong in this other world?" she had wondered. "I think that there's always been that struggle in many different respects."

She married in 1972, when she was twenty, around the same time hip-hop legend Kool Herc DJ'd his first block party. But she did not know that.

That night before the church event honoring the founding fathers and mothers of hip-hop, as the priest lies in bed, a car passes blasting Biggie on an otherwise silent night in the Bronx. Odd how quiet the projects can be. Then, as if the silence is too much, a girl will howl with laughter or rage or an engine will rev. But silence returns, even on Trinity Avenue, at the end.

THE ROSE

Friday, July 2, 2004

It was an Old Testament storm — " Noah's Ark type stuff," laughed D-Cross — complete with thunder and lightning and torrential rain. Everyone ran for cover and the mikes, speakers, and turntables were dragged inside the parish hall before there could occur a mass electrocution of the founding fathers and mothers of hip-hop.

Before the deluge, however, processions of children and neighbors from Trinity and from Forest Houses paraded around the streets to recorded raps by Mary Mary and Nas. "Girls jumped double-dutch jump rope and boys fired off firecrackers," Father Timothy recounted later. "Onlookers waved from high-rise PJs, and flower vendors, neighbors wondering what was up, students leaving Morris High School, helpful police officers — plainclothed and not — friends from the bodegas, dogs and cats, church people from Trinity, the diocese, and all around town — all joined at the Trinity hip-hop mass! God's love was proclaimed! Street and altar were joined!"

Pastoral hyperbole aside, Jahneen remembers being deeply moved that day. Before the music began, the rappers, DJs, and priest joined hands with the children and thugs of the South Bronx to pray on the asphalt of Trinity Avenue. As liturgical streamers whipped colorfully in the air around them, the priest gathered everyone together and gestured to the two dozen towers of Forest Houses rising starkly against the gathering storm. "This is our cathedral," he bellowed above the wind. "The South Bronx is our home. Hip-hop is our ministry. And God — God is our hope."

"I would have followed him anywhere after that prayer," Jahneen says softly. "And then the skies opened."

Before the first rhyme, the Trinity hip-hop mass raced back into the church. But everyone present remembers the power of that street prayer and a sense of something important taking root.

The first time the rap disciples took to the streets a few weeks earlier, it was a much simpler setup. DJ Old School Sam spun, but for the procession and for the service the priest had cued up raps on an old boom box. He kept checking his crib sheet to see which track to play: "Press 4" for the procession or "Press 2" for the sermon. It was low-tech and do-it-yourself, but no one seemed to mind. The first readings were John 1:14 and Tupac's poem, "The Rose that Grew from Concrete":

> *Did u hear about the rose that grew from a crack*
> *in the concrete*
> *Proving nature's laws wrong it learned 2 walk*
> *without having feet*
> *Funny it seems but by keeping its dreams*
> *it learned 2 breathe fresh air*
> *Long live the rose that grew from concrete*
> *When no one else even cared!*

During the service the impromptu congregation on the sidewalks shouted "Holler back!" and raps and prayers ended not with an "Amen" but with an emphatic, rowdy "Word!" Trinity Church had reached out, and Trinity Avenue had turned out.

"Everybody wanted to come out and see what was happening," Sam remembers. "There was people in a sense it was a little surprising to see out there — people from the projects — but they stood there the whole mass to see what's goin' on. They were given communion and from what I seen a lot of people were enjoying themselves. I wasn't getting negative vibes from anybody out there."

This definitely was not the church's usual crowd, although Mr. Warren, Marjorie Jones, Paula, and some others showed up to support the young people. The priest even remembers Paula dancing in the middle of the street she was not allowed to play in as a girl. No one wanted the day to end, but when it did, it was with a prayer, the same way it began.

Bishop Don Taylor, vicar bishop of the city of New York, a longtime Roberts family friend, was there that day and enthusiastically gave the first "Pontifical Hip-Hop Blessing" written by a twenty year-old local named Lamont Dean.

"God bless you and keep your back. Amen," intoned the bishop.

"Word!" the people responded.

"God make you a baller for his love at all times and to all peeps. Amen."

"Word!"

"God welcome you and yours into his church, always his homies. Amen."

"Word!"

The aging bishop's enthusiasm seemed to grow with that of the crowd, and his formality eased into the spirit of the day.

"God bless you with peace, joy, and def times forever. Amen."

"Word!"

"My sisters and brothers, all the posse of God, stay up!" Bishop Taylor proclaimed. "Keep your head up! Holler back! And go forth and tell it like it is! Amen!"

"WORD!"

The first Trinity hip-hop mass ended at dusk with roses. A Mexican family new to the South Bronx offered them as a gift to the congregation. The priest was reminded not only of Tupac's poem but also, fittingly, of the tradition of the Virgin of Guadalupe: "Where the poor are served, there roses bloom in December." Okay, so it was early June and the weather beautiful. No matter. He was a sucker for symbolic symmetry.

That first street mass in June was covered on the front page of the *Episcopal New Yorker*. Inside, Bishop Catherine Roskam wrote, "If Jesus were to come today, he would be a rapper." His would be a righteous freestyling, the priest agreed, a rap confronting the church's neglect, indifference, or irrelevance to "the least of these" in the hip-hop generation.

After such an auspicious beginning, spirits and hopes ran high for the July 2 mass honoring the founding fathers and mothers of hip-hop, and even rain of biblical proportions could not drown them.

Legends and pioneers of hip-hop showed up, including Kurtis Blow, Melle Mel of the Furious Five, Grandmaster Caz from the Cold Crush Brothers, DJ Lightning Lance and Waterbed Kev from the Fantastic Five. Cool Clyde even thought there was a chance the Godfather of Hip-Hop, Afrika Bambaataa, would come.

"Me, considering myself a student of hip-hop, it was an honor to be among them," D-Cross remembers. "It was interesting being in a church setting honoring hip-hop artists. Traditionally, churches are not accepting of hip-hop. At all."

It was Jahneen who brought D-Cross and the choir and musicians from St. Mark's Church in-the-Bowery. Her new partner helped supply much of the equipment. Cool Clyde and Sam from the towers would DJ again. Local young rappers, beatboxers, DJs, and MCs who showed up included Lamont, James, and DeSean, a breakdancer. They would return throughout the summer.

Two dozen clergy, wearing royal African kinte-cloth stoles in gold, brown, and black designed and made by Trinity's Altar Guild, stood beside enormous street speakers like those DJ Kool Herc used to use, flanking the stage serving as altar

rise. Bright streamers on long poles waved from each corner of
the stage.

At one point D-Cross rapped and beatboxed the Twenty-
Third Psalm, and the priest was astounded. When the Living
Instrument finished, he and the priest just looked at each
other. "I had never heard anything like it," Father Timothy
recalls. "It was beautiful, powerful. It was, in all honesty,
trance-like."

As D-Cross finished, Kurtis stepped forward, picked up the
microphone and started a praise rap. Many of those around the
stage remember seeing the King of Rap's "exultation." He was
so joyful, so full of spirit, like when he first started out breakdancing and rapping at house parties and park jams. The priest
had never seen the rapper before, but that first impression —
smiling, rapping, and exalting God — was how he would always
come to think of him.

But then Kurtis started going off program and all of Father Tim's meticulous planning went out the window. "Wait
a minute!" he thought, "That's not the way we Episcopalians
do it!" The party was on and the rappers were leading the way.
The priest was nervous.

Again, Bishop Roskam provided a soothing word. "Tim,"
she yelled into his ear over the remix and rap, "Let it happen."

"We were out there just having a good time one really nice
spring day," Kurtis remembers almost two years later. "It was
just an event to honor the people in the community and honor
the pioneers of hip-hop. When I showed up there with some
other old school cats, the vibe was just incredible coming into
the church. It's a beautiful church, Trinity. When we actually
did this thing, when we took to the street, the vibe, the people,
the Holy Spirit was in the house."

"I was optimistic at the end of the day," recalls D-Cross. "It
was a cool feeling."

Bishop Roskam presented each of the hip-hop legends and
pioneers with a Book of Common Prayer embossed with their
name in gold. Seeing her standing there in her gold crosses and

chains of office, someone remarked how the Episcopalians sure know their bling.

"I felt this anointing on the whole concept, the whole event," Kurtis remembers. "So I went to Father Tim — Poppa T — and I said, 'We need to do this thing every week, this is such a good thing.' It was supposed to be a one-time thing. And he said, 'You know, that's a great idea. I'm gonna think about it.'"

Afrika Bambaataa, the legendary Godfather of Hip-Hop, was a no-show that stormy day in July when the founding fathers and mothers of hip-hop brought Trinity Church and Trinity Avenue together, but toward the end of summer, Cool Clyde took the priest to Bambaataa's Zulu Nation headquarters in Harlem.

An imposing figure and leader even as a young man reigning over the new hip-hop scene, Bambaataa had only grown in stature over the decades just as he had grown in understanding. Bambaataa's credo for the organization he started in 1975 evolved to state in part: "The job of a Zulu is to survive in life. To be open-minded dealing with all walks of life upon this planet Earth and to teach [each] other truth (Knowledge, Wisdom, and Understanding). To respect those who respect them, to never be the aggressor or oppressor." The priest thought that sounded like common ground, and he was eager to meet the hip-hop legend.

They found Bambaataa napping. Back in the 1970s Bambaataa had dismissed the Christian "radical reverends" who came to speak to the street gangs. The priest wondered if he would "push aside" one more well-intentioned outsider. After a few pleasantries, however, the priest presented the towering figure with the Book of Common Prayer, Bambaataa's name gilded on the cover. They talked briefly about the Zulu Nation, the Episcopal Church, and the future of hip-hop. Nothing profound.

Then the two men, one a seminal and elemental force of hip-hop, the other a stranger in the hip-hop holy land, prayed together a prayer of thanksgiving. The audience lasted no more than ten minutes.

By then there had been seven Trinity hip-hop street services on consecutive Sundays.

⌒≈⌒

"Hip-hop is a gift from God," proclaims the King of Rap.

It was time to use that gift. During the summer of 2004 when he joined the Trinity hip-hop street masses, he had already been taking Bible classes out in L.A. Now he decided to take the next step, to take the advice of a pastor at a hip-hop ministry in Harlem who told him "you need to go back to school and learn to be a real minister if you're going to do this hip-hop church."

After meeting the priest he called Poppa T and appearing with the hip-hop ministry coalescing around Trinity, Kurtis was impressed by the spirit of what he had experienced and the sincerity of the priest. Sure, Father Timothy was a fish way out of water when it came to hip-hop. He seemed "somewhat punctilious," but he was "super intelligent," and they had God in common. Besides, the priest's Harvard degree made Kurtis feel as if there was some sound theology there. No doubt he was a "nerd," but he definitely knew his Bible and besides, he had a big heart. So what if he was over the top? He wanted to do the right thing. He was cool. Kurtis asked the priest to study with him, to help prepare him for confirmation and then ordination in the Episcopal Church.

Their first class was in August over lunch in a diner on Douglas Avenue, just off the Grand Concourse, where they talked church and Bible over *hamburguesas con queso* and Cokes. When they had finished, the priest had his own questions. He had given a great deal of thought to what Kurtis and Bishop Roskam had said and knew they were right. The street masses were too successful to let them simply end.

Nervously, he asked the rapper to be the music director for whatever this ministry was becoming. He figured it would never happen, fearing it would be a "high retail conversation." After all, this was the man who had helped put rap on the global charts and produced some of the biggest hip-hop acts of the 1980s. To his surprise, the rapper accepted immediately. For twenty minutes he brainstormed, and it was all the priest could do to keep up with the flow of ideas. In the end, not only did Kurtis refuse to accept any money for the position, he even bought the priest's lunch.

⸙

Kurtis had a busy tour schedule, but whenever he was in New York that summer he attended Trinity's high church service at 11:00 a.m. He cut quite the figure, decked out all in white, occasionally with rapper buddies in tow. The priest observed that he was not universally welcomed. More than a few long-time members of the congregation would pull Father Timothy aside to tell what they knew about the King of Rap's escapades and reputation. Not all the stories were true, but the ones that were gave the old guard plenty to arch their eyebrows over.

As a rule, the priest felt a pastoral duty to ignore gossip even if he personally enjoyed hearing the local "news." But the rapper had just started confirmation studies with him and he was "a child in the faith." He told the parishioners who had heard about the rapper's Idi Amin days, "If you're concerned about Kurtis, you should get to know him. Welcome him. Help him if you think he needs it."

Some, like Mr. Warren and Marjorie Jones, extended their hands. Paula did not know what to make of him. She would take a wait-and-see attitude. If you wait long enough, she thought, people cannot help but show you who they are.

⸙

In the sacristy to the left of the altar, his vestments neatly put away, Father Timothy thinks he is alone and gets down with his funky white self, dancing into the main sanctuary in his trademark Bermuda shorts and knee socks to the ubiquitous beat of "Lean Back," that summer's rap anthem by local luminary Fat Joe.

Only when the music ends does he notice Kurtis, early for their confirmation class, standing just inside the heavy wooden doors of the now quiet sanctuary.

"Brotherrrrrrrrr!" the priest bellows racing up the center aisle, making the word last as long as it takes him to stride the length of the church and take the rapper's hand, shaking it hard in both of his.

The two men are sitting on folding chairs at the head of the nave facing the doors beneath Trinity's vaulted beams. Their voices low, leaning toward one another in the otherwise silent church, they have been talking intimately for an hour about the history of the Episcopal Church and the nature of faith. But there is one more thing Father Timothy needs Kurtis to know before they can truly join together as brothers in hip-hop and Christ. He needs to tell him he is gay.

A month or two earlier, Father Timothy had tried to bring a rapper to Trinity from the Holy Hip Hop movement that began in Atlanta, but the man canceled when he read in the newspaper that the priest was the first openly gay man ordained in Alabama. That summer a local DJ had also backed out of Trinity's hip-hop street masses for the same reason. This second defection made the priest realize that the issue had to be confronted directly. He wondered how the King of Rap would deal with an openly gay priest. Would he also defect?

Choosing his words carefully, the priest tries to explain his apprehension. "I've been embraced and welcomed in beautiful ways by this church and by hip-hop," he offers, uncharacteristically subdued. "but my feelings have also been hurt by those in this church and in hip-hop."

In the spirit of their conversation he opened up. "Kurtis, you need to know I am openly gay," he said softly. The words seemed to echo in the church.

"You're gay, Father Tim?" The rapper seemed genuinely shocked.

"I am," was the reply. "I was made by God that way."

"You believe that?"

"I do."

"I didn't know that," Kurtis said quietly.

The muffled engine of the occasional car outside was the only sound.

"I don't want you to be hurt, Kurtis, by associating with me," the priest resumed. "People assume things. So you need to know this. And I don't want to be hurt, either. Most important, I don't want our young people to be hurt by misunderstandings over sexual identity."

"It was shocking," the rapper recalls. "*Shocking.* I'd never heard of ministers openly saying that they were homosexual. It was a shock to a lot of people."

That afternoon the two men resumed discussing the Bible. They did not talk about homosexuality in scripture or the elevation of Gene Robinson, a gay Episcopal priest, as the ninth bishop of the Diocese of New Hampshire earlier that year. The controversy had made national headlines and threatened to split the Episcopal Church. Instead, the priest says they talked about the commandments, painted in gold leaf around the sanctuary. He remembers telling the rapper his favorite was the love commandment. And then they sat for a few quiet moments in front of the altar, alone with their thoughts.

Kurtis remembers leaving Trinity that day committed to continuing the hip-hop services "because I'm a real hip-hopper and to show how hip-hop and God are so much alike. God does not care about denominations, or races, creeds, colors, ages, sexes, all that, right? Hip-hop is the same thing. It doesn't matter. Hip-hop is for everyone. We've been saying this since day one in 1972."

The priest and the rapper continued planning how they would bring their street ministry into Trinity Church that fall.

Kurtis decided he would watch Father Timothy's back because
that's hip-hop. Sure, the fact that the priest was gay came as a
huge shock, but he supported him. Hey, this was a middle-aged
white guy in shorts and knee socks walking the South Bronx.
Who is to say which is more shocking?

JESUS AT THE BRONX

Sunday, October 3, 2004

At the first burst of rap coming from inside Trinity Church, old men standing in front of the JCJ Supermarket Corporation bodega peer through the gathering dusk to see where the music is coming from. Young guys hanging around outside Forest Houses look confused, and their girlfriends laugh as the beat of the inaugural HipHopEMass monthly rap service carries beyond the open doors and into the street. The church looks no different from the sidewalk below where people shake their heads at this unexpected and not entirely understandable new turn. Trinity, it seems, is making noise.

As Jahneen sings Kanye West's "Jesus Walks," Kurtis, Paradox, the Missionary Men, and Father Tim follow the children carrying the golden crucifix and swinging the incense burner up the center aisle between the pews. Beneath the statue of Mary, the newly formed HipHopEMass band has cut loose. D-Cross is front and center shouting out, "God is in the house! God is in the house!"

The Trinity hip-hop masses in the streets that summer of 2004 were officially reborn inside as HipHopEMass.org in October that year. The EMass disciples adopted "Jesus of the Bronx," the children's immediate choice, for the ministry's logo on the website and on thousands of posters, hand cards, and mass cards announcing the weekly services. This Jesus was rendered in bright purple, pink, and yellow, a crown of thorns on his head and rivulets of blood on his face. Below the image in gothic script always were the words, "The Word was made flesh and dwelt in the 'Hood."

"We welcome everybody!" the priest declares expansively. "That's what the 'E' stands for: God loves everybody everywhere, excellently, extravagantly, forevermore!"

The front rows were filled with children from Forest Houses and the surrounding streets with the older folks farther back, away from the speakers. In a side pew, Marjorie Jones has seen nothing like this in over thirty years of worshipping at Trinity. Dressed for church, one of what the priest calls her "hats of attitude" poised becomingly on her perfectly set hair, she tries to clap along, but the music is so loud she decides it is pointless. She is glad there are children in the church again. But, goodness, it's loud.

Father Timothy, the heavy sleeves of his Episcopal vestments swinging as he claps in the children's processional, shouts out the front door to a few curious spectators peering inside the sanctuary to come join them. Turning to process down Trinity's center aisle, he feels surprisingly bashful, not entirely sure what God has in store, but seeing the rappers and the children celebrating so naturally, so at home in the church, he shakes off any self-consciousness and follows the rapper carrying high the Gospel Book.

D-Cross is beatboxing in front of the church. A red satin "HipHopEMass" altar cloth covers the Tiffany Eucharist table. Off to the side, singing backup next to the band, Jahneen smiles broadly. People straggle in from the street, first a father leading a boy and girl by the hand, then a teenage girl in an oversized sweatshirt. A young man carrying a toddler, her head covered in pink barrettes, takes a seat in back.

"His love don't stop!" D-Cross is rapping now.

The congregation tonight is made up mostly of people in their early twenties and younger but one of the Missionary Men is surprised to see among the rows people from the neighborhood and church, "like fifty-something or older than that, like sixty-something." Five boys, ranging from about twelve to fifteen years old, jostle each other in a side pew behind Sister Marjorie. Opposite, to the left of the nave, three church ladies in floral dresses and beauty parlor coifs sit quietly. One of them begins to clap along with the music. Her friends lean back and look at her sideways with broad, comical skepticism, but when the congregation rises, they do too.

D-Cross calls out "God is great!" and the congregation responds, "All o' the time!"

"God is GREAT!"

"All o' the TIME!"

The service follows the traditional format, but the music and lexicon are hip-hop. Jahneen serves as MC at the altar, leading the call and response that ends, "We praise you, we bless you! We represent our love to you!"

The priest then recites the Beatitudes as the Living Instrument scratches behind him. Then the beatboxer prays, "May God bless our city, bless the prisoners, those in pain, those in need. Bless bless y'all." He starts to freestyle, turning the prayer into a rap. "Bless bless, y'all . . . " The band joins in and soon the church almost vibrates with bass lines and beats.

Then Kurtis takes up the microphone, rapping and moving up the center aisle:

There's a devastation in our nation
A ball of confusion, we need a Church revolution. . . .
Paid by Christ, it's time to share the Gospel with the
> *whole generation*
Emancipation of a Nation. . . .

Two of the ladies in floral prints leave discreetly. Another walks right up the center aisle to the exit. Everyone else is on their feet, clapping and moving to the beat. The freestyling winds down and the band moves into the soft R&B riffs of the classic "Change Is Gonna Come." It's the priest's turn to preside over the Eucharist.

"All are welcome at the table, baptized or not," he says, inviting the people forward. Seeing the ladies leave, he adds, "Those who don't join our circle aren't getting all the love in the room."

The boys stop jostling and step forward for communion. All the children line up, Sister Marjorie too, everyone in fact except for some church ladies who remain seated in the safety of the pew.

Glory steps forward, eyes raised, and points to heaven, then to the altar surrounded by rappers, kids from Forest Houses, robed priests, white and black, worshipping together. When the last person returns to his seat, Poppa T raises his hands for the Pontifical Hip-Hop Blessing.

The church, full of music and dancing and clapping just moments before, is now still.

" . . . My sisters and brothers, all the posse of God, stay up!" he says reverently in his best hip-hop. "Keep your head up, holler back, and go forth and tell it like it is. Amen."

"Word," respond the rappers standing beside him.

"Amen," he says again, louder this time.

"Word!" the rappers shout, joined now by most of the congregation.

"Amen!" The priest is practically shouting now.

"Word!"

"Amen!"

"WORD!"

⤜⤚

It was like family, the HipHopEMass crew. That's how Glory felt after his very first service. "I was growing more with the Lord and in the way to pray, learning in the process who I was," he said. "It was crazy. The experience was love. I was touching another side of me I never thought existed before the HipHopEMass."

"People did come to me afterward and say, 'What you guys are doing is great,'" Paradox remembered. " 'You need to keep doing it.' A lot of people were enthusiastic and left with a positive impression. Also in that community, I mean if you want to call it the ghetto, it's what people call the ghetto, it's the 'hood. A lot of kids that don't go to church — we just know they don't go to church — were there."

"It kind of broadened their view on God," added Jahdiel. "It didn't limit it to a certain type of worship, a certain type of expression."

Rock nodded his head in agreement. "There was just a whole bunch of different religions and every ethnicity there just checking it out, seeing what it was doing. So it was a good start. Some people left saying, 'Oh, this is weird,' but other people left saying, 'This is interesting, very interesting.'"

"I was shivering inside," recalled Kurtis. "I felt the Holy Spirit inside the room."

Despite the Holy Spirit and the enthusiasm of the young rappers and MCs, however, Kurtis still had his professional standards.

"It was a horrible production," he laughingly confessed. "There was only forty to fifty people, that was it. We had a big, huge sound system and everything was feeding back. The microphones were just horrible. Everything went wrong. But people came back double the next week. So it was a huge success. Not by my standards but by God's standards."

※

From there things began to happen very fast. That first year the HipHopEMass crew fielded invitations from Massachusetts to Texas, appearing at correction facilities, women's shelters, street events, and church conventions. Aside from eighteen masses at street and altar at Trinity Church and on Trinity Avenue, the rap disciples held seven more services in five cities in four different states.

Soon rappers from outside the South Bronx were joining them, more than twenty in all. By the end of the year, more than five thousand people had celebrated the HipHopEMass and the ministry received the "Blessed Are the Peacemakers Award" from the World Council of Churches.

The ministry was a success, but the priest wondered if his question to Bishop Sisk that inspired all of this — are we legitimate? — might not have been loaded in ways he was only beginning to grasp. What does it mean to be legitimate in the street and at the altar? Frankly, he was self-conscious standing up there, both because he was still a student of hip-hop and also because some of the hip-hop disciples were still in many ways students of the faith.

Early on, during the summer street masses and with the permission of the bishop, they had decided to diverge from the Episcopalian lectionary that determined each service. Too many young people and adults were unfamiliar with Bible stories, even what the priest considered to be "the big ones." The whole point of taking the altar to the street would be defeated if the church continued to go about its business in the same way, not caring whether the people understood or followed. Instead, during the seven summer masses he had put the lectionary aside and highlighted stories of creation, the exodus, the prophets, Jesus, Mary, discipleship, and love. It was a beginning but was it legitimate?

He needed to pray. Didn't he always say that the rappers will show us the way, that the rappers will lead us? So how come he still felt as if he had to control everything, to make sure this ministry could not be criticized as a gimmick, or "that old-time religion" in hip-hop drag. He didn't want the children he was trying to reach to see it as just a cheesy imitation of something real.

Hip-hop was prophetic. He believed that. "Hip-hop is hope!" he said once when asked how he, a middle-aged, white, gay priest sporting too many pounds and too much stress, could lead a hip-hop ministry. "More than any social and community organization, more than most churches, synagogues or mosques, hip-hop represents hope to generations of our young people in the Bronx, in New York, and throughout the United

States. A deaf ear to this reality is a closed heart and mind to our children and young people, to their hopes, visions, and dreams."

He had been pleased with his answer but, still, the question had hurt.

If he could just step back and let the rappers lead, then the HipHopEMass could speak to a whole generation that hasn't heard the good news. It could be a revelation and a promise to the Hip-Hop Nation, offering a real God, a redeeming love, and new life. But it had to come from the rappers themselves. They were the disciples, and only they could tell how the Word was made flesh and dwelt in the 'hood.

But he had a hard time stepping back. He knew it. His ego sometimes got in the way. Okay, often got in the way. At a meeting of provincial leaders of the Episcopal Church in Albany, the first time the HipHopEMass crew had ventured beyond the South Bronx, he had stood front and center, D-Cross, Jahneen, and the Missionary Men rapping on the sidelines. Afterward, the attention and praise were more gratifying than he would have imagined. Expecting another compliment, he had asked someone he admired what he had thought of the service. "I think it's a very fine worship," the man had said, "but there's one thing."

"What's that?" the priest had asked eagerly.

"Father, you need to get out of the way."

It was a painful moment. The experience had put him on his knees, and when he got up again, the rappers stood beside him at the Eucharist table. They were the messengers, their rhymes became the sermons, and their remix of gospel and hip-hop created a new theology, the best of what Christianity and hip-hop could be. They challenged the church and they smashed the false idols of gangsta rap. They were legitimate. He would follow their lead. He would try.

The Reverend Timothy Holder was not unaccustomed to trying to win people over, first unsuccessfully as a political operative for the Democratic Party in the South working on the Mondale and Dukakis presidential campaigns, then with better luck as the first openly gay priest ordained in the diocese of Alabama. His greatest challenge as a Christian, as a gay man, and as a religious leader, however, was before him. He had to win over the children in the PJs.

Come rain or shine, he continued to walk his parish. He didn't always get the response he wanted, but it didn't matter, he told himself. It was a start. Sometimes Glory came with him, and together they passed out the Jesus of the Bronx mass cards, or Glory would rap some while he made his pitch to come on by the church.

He would waylay boys racing down the sidewalk and corral them into an impromptu prayer. He would greet women on their stoops who looked like they would rather be left alone. He was introducing his church to the 'hood and his 'hood to the church and so he couldn't be shy. As if that had ever been his problem.

The neighborhood seemed to be getting used to it, though. Anita Brown, a diminutive woman with hennaed hair living on Trinity Avenue, shrugged, "I'm a Catholic, I go to St. Augustus, but I enjoy the EMass. . . . I'm not gonna change my religion but I go and I bring my child."

At Western Beef near the projects, a young clerk recognized him — "I know you!" — and asked the priest to bless her rainbow necklace. Glory's father took to introducing himself on the streets as the priest's "security" by way of thanks for all he was doing for his son.

Striding boldly onto a basketball court between two Forest Houses towers on an early fall afternoon, the priest grabbed the ball midpass, asking disingenuously with that thick Tennessee drawl, "You guys like rap?"

In the projects, a flamboyant white gay man with a clerical collar is still a flamboyant white gay man. But rather than

getting beat down, the priest invited the b-ballers to the Friday
night rap service at Trinity and, in a miracle to rival the part-
ing of the Red Sea, managed to get all nine boys to bow their
heads inside the key and pray, ignoring their embarrassment
and giggles. "Amen, Word," he finished, then walked on as if
leaving a church potluck.

"Hip-hop respects guts," he explained. "We could get shot
at. But we've got work to do."

꙳

Not once in over 150 recorded tracks had Kurtis Blow Walker
used profanity. Not once. Even when he was running with Ike
and Sly and getting a rep as the Idi Amin of music, even as
the gangster life was taking over hip-hop, he never swore or
degraded women in his raps. Even on the songs he produced
for others, he never let the artists curse. He wasn't sure if it
was because of God, but he definitely knew it was because of
hip-hop, the unity, peace, and love he believed it stood for. His
personal life might have been another story, but even when he
had not been true to God at least he had always been true to
hip-hop.

But he was almost ashamed of it now. He no longer even
wanted to tell people he was one of the pioneers of rap because
of the thug image. When people learned he was a rapper, he
imagined they were collecting their purses and touching their
wallets. What was good and spiritual about how it all started,
its righteous cry from oppressed people, was silenced. Now it
was all foul language and fronting as "gangstas."

After he had renewed his covenant with God in the early
1990s, his music had not really changed. It was not until
joining up with Father Timothy and the HipHopEMass that
he began rapping for Christ. It was a revelation to him that
hip-hop and God could work together. It made him realize he
wanted to be a minister. Even if no one was listening, he believed once again, finally, he had something to say. It was why
he began confirmation classes with Father Timothy. He came

from the world of hip-hop but hardly anyone was talking to that world about God. And he wanted to save souls. Bottom line. He wanted to bring his world — the world he had helped create — the Word of God.

For him there had always been a close relationship between a rapper and a preacher. Maybe that is what he had in common with Father Timothy. It certainly wasn't style. But he loved the way the priest worked his own church rap, preaching and singing scripture in that pure tenor voice. He believed preachers were the most passionate of all orators, coming across with a lot of fire. This ministry brought together his passion for God and his gift for rap. This was his new calling, another first in a career of firsts. Just as he had once pioneered hip-hop, he could put his talents and gifts into pioneering a new way to hear God.

"Jesus told stories people related to," says Kurtis about those early days, looking up from his Bible before a service. "And different kinds of stories for different kinds of people, stories or parables that related to each segment of different cultures. If he was around today, he probably still would do the same thing. That's what we tried to do at the HipHopEMass — present the gospel and God in language that the kids can understand."

And there was something else. He couldn't help thinking about the Exodus, how Moses led the Hebrews out of bondage to Pharaoh. But after they left Egypt, where did they go? Into the wilderness. The desert. And for how long? Forty years. By his way of thinking, hip-hop had been around for about thirty-three years. Right now it seemed to him as if the Hip-Hop Nation was lost in the wilderness. They were all out in the wilds, looking for the Promised Land, for someplace to rest, for something more. They hadn't found it in money or sex or any of the golden calves of thug life. Thirty-three years is a long time to wander without finding your way. It seemed to him that it was time the lost children of hip-hop "got our act together."

Some thought of it as a performance, a gimmick, or a gig. But along with the rapping, scratching, and beatboxing, there was always preaching, prayer, and blessing. Whenever he heard criticism or confusion or questioned the ministry himself, the priest would ask what is the purpose of the church today? Who will speak for the thugs? He knew that this hip-hop ministry was not all that the church is or should be, but he believed whole-heartedly that it was an essential, integral part. In fact, the church could not be the church without it because it was the Word, the flesh, the beat, and the love of God for a new people in this time.

If the whole purpose of liturgy is to enter into a deeper encounter with God, to praise him and know him, then what is the point of rites and traditions that keep some of his children at arm's length or actively send them away? God wants us to know him, the priest was convinced, and he will speak to us at the right time and in a language we can understand.

As Bishop Roskam wrote in the *Episcopal New Yorker* after the very first street mass, "Can it be that liturgy can be expressed faithfully within such diverse forms? Such was the question in the sixteenth century when the church decided to leave Latin for the language of the people. The answer in our tradition is that liturgy cannot be expressed faithfully *without* such diverse forms."

No, the priest thought, hip-hop wasn't the devil. Instead, it holds the church accountable, just as the church holds hip-hop accountable. Bringing rap into Trinity was challenging, he knew. It — and he — was earning the wrath of the orthodox in both the pews and the streets who found themselves in the unlikely position of being challenged on their own turf for the soul of the church and the nature of hip-hop.

But he also dared to dream that the Friday night rap services could serve as a ministry of transcendence, for the individual, for the church, for the hip-hop generations, one with the potential to carry far beyond the length of Trinity Avenue or the confines of the South Bronx into the very spirit of worship, the nature of faith, and the heart of the thug life.

By bringing hip-hop into the church, the HipHopEMass crew didn't just challenge Trinity's more traditional church-goers to open their doors and hearts, however. It was also a challenge to the easy piety of anyone, Philistine or not, for whom religious observance replaces the hard work of faith. Kurtis had said on more than one occasion that faith is a process, not a dogma. The church lives only when it seeks to respond to the prophet's call to do justice, love kindness, and walk humbly, or as Jesus put it, to love God with all our heart and mind and soul and our neighbor as ourselves.

Well, the priest reasoned, both the thug life and the Eucharist demand to know who is our neighbor. He could not get around it: the emphatic answer is "Everyone." Thugs, hip-hoppers, and gangbangers — the lepers, Samaritans, and im-poverished of today, the very people Jesus came for. The Word of God and the words of rap upon which the HipHopEMass is based are a prophetic voice, asking, do we love our liturgy and traditions more than we love our neighbor?

They ask, "Who will speak for the thugs?" and it challenges the church to respond, "We will." No, the priest thinks — more than that: it challenges the church to recognize, "We *are* the thugs."

OUTRAGE

"Outrage," was Paula's immediate response. "I couldn't believe it! I was outraged."

It was time to bring those who had attended the hip-hop street services into the church, the priest had decided. That July at the conclusion of the children's hip-hop summer program D-Cross was leading, he arranged for a graduation ceremony at Trinity's traditional 11:00 a.m. Sunday service. Taking the altar to the street had been such a great success it only seemed natural to next bring the street to the altar.

"Let us ask God in all vernaculars, tongues, and cultures for leadership, courage, and vision," he had proclaimed by way of introducing the young people from what they now called the Hip Hop Vacation Church School. "Let us sing the new song of Jesus Christ in the language of our younger generation!"

Kids with liturgical streamers on poles paraded between the pews, and someone rapped the Twenty-Third Psalm: *"The Lord is all that, I need for nothing...."* At first the priest thought people were "joyous," but when DeSean Wilson started break-dancing in front of the altar with others from the 'hood, several people walked out. When he and the children from the street services recessed to Nas's hit "I Can," which features children rapping and shouting the words "I Know I Can / Be What I Wanna Be" over a bass-heavy sample of Beethoven's *Für Elise,* he realized those looks on the faces of the older parishioners weren't joyous at all.

The complaints started immediately: the service looked like a parade or picnic; too many kids were "unkempt" and looked like they walked in right off the streets; dancing did not belong in the church; the music was too loud and, besides, it was hip-hop. The Roberts family, in particular, was deeply offended. All this came second-hand, of course. No one complained to the priest directly.

"Father Tim is so full of vim and vigor, he likes to share everything," offers Marjorie Jones. "He thought it would be a good thing to bring the children into the traditional congregation to share what they had learned, but people thought that was going to be the new format for Sunday and they didn't like it. I wouldn't have either. But they lost sight of the fact that this was a one-time thing."

Father Timothy claims he was told by Mr. Warren and Lillas Bogle, the church wardens, that the negative feedback was coming from only a half dozen parishioners in their seventies and eighties, but they were a powerful group, including Lucille Roberts and her daughter.

Paula had not been at Trinity that morning, but when she heard about what had happened, she could not believe it. She did not keep her outrage to herself. "I think that Tim was trying to force the issue," she says, "and he saw that it was completely demolished by everybody."

Whether opposed by a group of six influential parishioners or by "everybody," combining the high Episcopalian liturgy with the hip-hop mass that one Sunday morning was a turning point not just for Father Timothy's relationship to his congregation but for the future of the young ministry.

"It is a very traditional church," Paula explains. "And bringing this sort of very radical change into the service, or into the church, was something people could not...." Her voice trails off.

She felt somehow betrayed. She had been instrumental in getting the priest to come to Trinity, even traveling with Marjorie Jones to Alabama to persuade him. She had supported him with the vestry, been open to his new ideas, including the street masses. Hadn't she attended at least three of them herself? Even though the church leadership was left out of the planning, even though she was not entirely sold on the idea, she had given the priest the benefit of the doubt. But this was too much.

Maybe hip-hop could help rebuild the church. She didn't know. What she did know is that being open to new ideas did not mean disrespecting church traditions or the needs of the longtime congregation. She also knew the polite West Indian parishioners of her mother's generation would never confront the priest. If there were something the priest wanted, even if it offended them, they would be silent about it. Well, she wasn't afraid of the priest. She had been raised to speak her mind, and it was in her nature to take charge. So it fell to her. She had to speak up. This was a house of worship — of *worship* — after all.

⌐≈ᴗ

There was something about hip-hop that felt familiar and resonated with his own Deep South experience. Maybe it was the visionary myth-making surrounding Afrika Bambaataa and the other architects of hip-hop that would have been familiar to Twain or Capote or O'Connor, Southern raconteurs who never let the facts get in the way of a good story. Sometimes facts just slowed down the truth. Vision was more important when there is a whole new world to create.

Bambaataa, Kurtis, Cool Clyde, and many others gave rise to a culture and a style that reflected their world around them but were still inspired by a world no one had yet ever seen. Imagining a whole new creation was the work of prophets. The priest believed that. The old definition of faith in scripture seemed apt: "Faith is the substance of things hoped for and the evidence of things unseen."

Hip-hop began as the substance of a generation's hopes, a generation that had been discarded and forgotten. It was for them, and for a time, the evidence of a life worth living and a world worth living in. The priest believed it could be again. In the face of evidence to the contrary, hip-hop's archetypes, traditions, and larger-than-life characters could help remake the world for those the church was now discarding or forgetting. All that was needed was the sixth element of hip-hop: Spirituality. The missing ingredient, he believed, was God.

⤳

God's rappers, beatboxers, and DJs created a hip-hop service that October at the World Council of Churches Conference in Atlanta. There D-Cross, Kurtis, Jahneen, and Father Timothy met other Christians building hip-hop ministries all over the country.

They also met the young Toronto-based rapper Defy the Odds. D.O. had made hip-hop history in 2003 when he claimed the Guinness World Record for the World's Longest Freestyle, rapping nonstop for eight hours and forty-five minutes. He was no novelty act, getting respect from Chuck D. of Public Enemy, the magazine *XXL* as one of rap's new breed, and soon from the South Bronx crew as one of the hip-hop disciples.

The priest began to realize that what they were doing in the South Bronx was part of a larger hip-hop church movement taking root in small towns, big cities, and different denominations across the country. It gave him some comfort to know that they were not alone in following this calling to preach the gospel to many nations, including the Hip-Hop Nation.

He had long conversations with rappers and DJs aligned with the much larger Holy Hip Hop movement, and although everyone was friendly, their exclusionary hip-hop gospel troubled him. Others, like Jahdiel and Monk of the Missionary Men, would later comment on how the Holy Hip Hop contingent kept rapping about loving God but didn't exactly have many specifics in their lyrics about how to do that.

Rap trio the Remnant, formed by "Just-John" Jordan, Adam Beane, and Niles Gray while all three were still undergraduates at Morehouse College in Atlanta, connected with the South Bronx crew. They gave the priest one of their CDs. "We call ourselves the Remnant but we're really the Nerds," explained Just-John, the unofficial spokesman of the trio.

The three friends agreed to stay in touch and accepted Father Timothy's invitation to join the HipHopEMass crew when they traveled to the South the following year.

Before leaving Atlanta and heading back to the South Bronx, Just-John christened Father Timothy "Poppa T." The priest took to the name immediately as a sign of acceptance and it set him free as a hip-hop priest. The moniker stuck, as did the Remnant's alliance with Trinity's HipHopEMass.

"Poppa T's sincerity, his sacrifices to reach people, is something we had to sign on with," Just-John explains, sitting in a motel breakfast room after a long drive to worship with the Trinity crew. "He has that hip-hop sincerity and he knows Jesus is life."

⌒⊰⌒

The priest returned to Trinity as Poppa T, with a new energy and sense of calling. Every Sunday night at 6:30 p.m. that first October, the pews at Trinity were filled with rap and praise. The enthusiasm of the new hip-hop crew coalescing around the church took the priest by surprise. What was supposed to be a one-time street mass became a "nice summer program for the kids," and then a full-fledged outreach ministry. It was Kurtis who pushed the priest to think beyond the summer after they conducted their first prison mass in August.

"He was ready to get things going and I was thinking, this is great, we're gonna have a great summer, but I had no intention of keeping this thing going," Poppa T confesses with a huge grin. "I had to get on with being a 'priest.'" He speaks the word with bombast and sly Southern quotes.

"If not for Kurtis Blow," he says, "we would not have begun our weekly masses in October 2004."

"And it was great." Kurtis also recalls that time with a smile in his voice. "It was wonderful."

Paula did not agree. Others, including some members of the church vestry, didn't like what they heard or saw either. Even though the priest never tried to bring hip-hop back into the traditional Sunday morning services again, returning the HipHopEMass to Sunday evenings, the very fact that the ministry was taking root at Trinity was upsetting.

In dozens of informal conversations, some whispered, some not, people wanted to know where all this hip-hop was coming from all of a sudden. The priest wanted to know where Trinity had been for the last thirty-odd years.

A few longtime members, like Mr. Warren, Marjorie Jones, and Lillas Bogle, senior warden of the vestry, tried hard to understand and welcome the new faces and new sound. But for many of the older congregation, the HipHopEMass was too loud, too irreverent, and most likely blasphemous. When the vestry took up the question, Mr. Warren stated that he was pleased they were exploring how to reach out to the children and young adults in the neighborhood.

"The older members of our church are dying out," he said in his role as Trinity's junior warden. "For our church to grow, we need to bring people in. The kids look forward to Sunday nights."

Paula had been willing to let Father Timothy — she refused to call him Poppa T — try out some new ideas, to do outreach his way. But this was simply the wrong way.

Didn't rappers glorify violence, drugs, easy sex, and gangs, everything their faith stood against? How could rap possibly glorify God or lead these children to him? And how could this new priest open their doors and invite the worst part of the world into their church? Trinity had always stood apart. Now the street and the altar were joined. And as far as Paula, the majority of the vestry, and several of the traditionalists were concerned, it was the street, not the altar, that now seemed to be ruling the house of God.

"I was told that never before were there so many local neighborhood children at Trinity," Poppa T recalls. "But their presence caused some discomfort. . . . From the beginning there was a problem welcoming children and young people with the HipHopEMass night program. But if we're not gonna have Hispanic children or African American children, or hip-hop in the South Bronx USA, just what are we gonna have?"

He tried not to show it, but the priest was riled by the criticism and cold-shoulder toward the children who led the youth service. And, yes, he felt he was unfairly criticized himself. He wasn't a fool. He knew hip-hop was characterized by gross commercialism, images of violence, and lyrics of degradation toward women, gays, and others. Does that mean the church runs away, scared? No! Just as Jesus met people on their own turf in his day, the church needed to meet hip-hop on the street and proclaim God's hope and God's love in the middle of the pain and confusion. It was the archbishop of Canterbury himself who, when speaking about folk customs, declared, "Our task is to 'church' these sentiments, not belittle them."

He realized that Paula, perhaps more than the others, instinctively if not consciously recognized what hip-hop producer and commentator Bill Stephney once observed: "Hip-hop was not just a 'fuck you' to white society, it was a 'fuck you' to the previous Black generation as well." The one-time member of SNCC, the woman whose parents raised her on the Anglo-Catholic tradition and the NAACP, was not about to let anyone get away with that.

But weren't Paula's generation and that of her father and mother letting these young people down by preferring incense and organ hymns to their presence in the house of God? As for the cuss words, well, that was an obvious objection. Profanity did not belong anywhere near his ministry or altar. But people had to get beyond these easy criticisms to address the real problems and find what was holy and powerful about hip-hop. Besides, as Quincy Jones said, he was just not willing to throw away two or three generations of our youth because of a curse word here and there.

No, Trinity had to wake up, get real, and love a little bit more and a whole lot better. Otherwise, it might not be here over the next 140 years.

⬧

El Presidente Salvadorean Restaurant is right across from New York Presbyterian Hospital, where Paula had put in another long day. The priest had asked to speak with her after receiving her email about the Sunday Hip Hop Vacation Bible School youth service. Together perhaps they could stem the growing controversy over the hip-hop ministry. While Paula may not have been serving on the vestry, she was certainly looked to for leadership. Longtime members still turned to a Roberts for guidance even if they were no longer in charge. She agreed to meet with Father Tim.

Dinner was the only time free in her tight schedule, and he agreed to drive the old Ford Taurus across the bridge. When she slid into the booth, she pushed the menu aside and got right down to business.

"I am very sad about all this," she began. "I think there may be ways we can make this work."

Quickly, however, before the waiter came to take their order, the priest remembers Paula demanding that hip-hop be kept out of Trinity and the new ministry be dropped. There was, in his recollection, no attempt to "make this work." It soon became clear that this was not a conversation but a confrontation. Paula had come to dictate terms, not negotiate.

"I expressed my . . . ," Paula hesitates while searching for the right word " . . . my disagreement with bringing hip-hop into the church because we have a very traditional way of worship which I felt should be maintained. I felt that way for myself, and I also felt that way for the congregants."

She told him that he needed to respect the traditional Anglo-Catholic way of worship. The priest responded with some heat that he was honoring their tradition, but rather than just emphasizing what was beautiful and traditional about the Anglican prefix, the diversity inherent in the Catholic suffix deserved equal time. He was not about to close the doors of Trinity to the neighborhood where it stood. He said he would not put up a "Not Welcome" sign on the front gate. In fact, he had every intention of throwing it wide open and, as he had preached on many occasions, letting the children overwhelm them.

Paula could not help thinking this had as much if not more to do with the priest's ambition as with the children of Forest Houses. "My feelings toward Tim began to shift because I felt Tim was doing a lot of things — not just this — for his own grandiosity. . . . I think this was a way that he could build his own empire, to be very honest."

The priest dismissed such talk, believing the problem was more about personal power than liturgical purity. After more than fifty years in positions of authority and influence at Trinity, someone was telling a Roberts "no."

"It was from this time that I believe she became concerned mostly if not exclusively about 'control,'" the priest says. "Probably for the first time ever, her authority had been challenged in regard to the future direction of 'her family's' church. Change was at hand!"

The idea was ludicrous, according to Paula. "If some people see this as a power struggle simply because they don't like the response they get, then so be it. For me, this was a simple call for leadership." The priest was ignoring his responsibilities, as far as she was concerned.

"He didn't put as much into the rest of the church and the congregation as he did into hip-hop," she recalls telling him. "And definitely the congregation was going down, finances

were going down, and I don't feel that he was paying attention to that the way that a rector should. He was just putting
all his energy into building hip-hop."

For the priest's part, he was puzzled by the charge that he
was ignoring his duties and the longtime parishioners. "When
you bury people, you get to know that family pretty good," he
said. "I have close friends here. I think I'll have a legacy among
the aged here, but I also hope I have a legacy of helping this
parish move into the future, stand up for itself, and welcome
new people."

The priest and the daughter of Trinity were at an impasse.
She could not understand why he refused to see that hip-hop
was an affront to Trinity and did not belong in the church.
He was appalled that the woman who as a little girl had felt
so isolated and different when confronted with the lives and
customs of her rich classmates could not find it in her heart to
welcome children just as they are.

Parishioners would soon take sides. While some would see
the growing rift between them as a clash between two strong
personalities with competing personal agendas, it would not
be entirely accurate, even if that was how they sometimes saw
it themselves. Paula and the priest believed, each in their own
way, that they were being true to their best understanding of
God's will, of what their faith called for and what worship could
and should be.

As far as the priest was concerned, he needed little more
evidence than the sight and sound of children from the PJs in
church sporting T-shirts reading, "Jesus is my Homeboy." Hip-
hop was not going away. He would not let his church bury its
head in the sand. They were called to welcome the neighbors
and move forward.

For Paula, worship was a way to reach deep and allow God
to enter her soul. That did not include a turntable, a backbeat, or a young man spinning on his head in the aisle in
front of the altar. She would do anything to protect the Trinity she loved and the rites and liturgy she was born into, and

she was convinced this priest and his hip-hop ministry were destroying them.

The dinner ended without either one taking more than a bite or two. The woman who had been among his first allies, the priest now realized, was "in no frame of mind to work with me or say anything positive about hip-hop."

It was not until the following year that Paula would return any of the priest's calls.

⤬

They all lived for Sunday evenings that October. Jahneen, Kurtis, the Missionary Men, D-Cross, the musicians in the first line-up of the HipHopEMass band, they all came from different parts of the city to the South Bronx to worship and raise the roof. Poppa T was working hard, and working everyone else hard too, but so far the enthusiasm and faith of the HipHopEMass crew was carrying them all. For the time being, they could ignore the haters and critics in both the church and the hip-hop community and even the differences among themselves. They had a congregation to build.

Then one Monday night in November after one of their biggest services yet, on the eve of the election that would return George W. Bush to the White House, the priest got a voicemail message from Kurtis.

"Father Tim," said the voice. "This is Kurtis Blow. I don't agree with the leadership of your church. I won't be back." Kurtis was about to establish his own hip-hop ministry.

THE WEAPON GOD GAVE US

Over a period of several months, since December 2004, there had already been four big vestry meetings and hundreds of informal discussions about the HipHopEMass. The meetings often became heated and Poppa T was angry with himself for allowing discussions to devolve into personal attacks, mostly against him. However, Mr. Warren, Lillas Bogle, Marjorie Jones, and other longtime members of Trinity were also harshly criticized for supporting the hip-hop ministry and the rappers. The insults and invective made it impossible to have a rational discussion about hip-hop in the church.

The church that had survived near-demolition, civil unrest, infernos, gang warfare, and the virulence of drugs and poverty was coming apart over hip-hop.

There were two main factions, those who supported the hip-hop ministry and those who wanted it out of Trinity completely. As Mr. Warren saw it, Father Tim (he too just couldn't bring himself to call him Poppa T) helped bring in more young people, but folks didn't want them at Trinity if it was going to involve rap. They couldn't or wouldn't understand that what the priest and the rappers were doing was different. "As soon as the older folks heard 'hip-hop,' everyone was turned off," he said. "They didn't bother to hear the EMass part."

Only a small number were willing to take to heart the parable of the fig tree the priest chanted the morning after the siege, waiting to see what kind of fruit the ministry would bear. Foremost among them was Joe Barrett, Lucille Roberts's cousin, who seemed torn between more than fifty years of traditional worship at Trinity and his desire to see his church enter a new day and young hearts. He was in the difficult position of supporting Father Roberts's widow and daughter, who were his kin, and wanting to find out whether the children could be churched and if the church could make room for the new in order to grow.

After that Sunday the previous summer when breakdancers and rappers overwhelmed the traditional morning mass, Paula began writing several passionate emails and letters to the diocese, various bishops, Trinity's vestry, and the congregation about the matter. She believed she spoke for those who would not or could not speak for themselves. She believed she was defending what was best about Trinity and the Anglo-Catholic tradition. "I love Trinity," she said. "I saw that it and the tradition of what my father and others built was being destroyed. So I needed to protect my church and family."

Meanwhile, the priest and the rappers were making headlines wherever they traveled and being interviewed on radio and TV. Finally, Geraldo's TV show came calling. This infuriated Paula and some of the others even more. They believed the good name of Trinity was being destroyed by the association. The priest was giving the wrong impression of what they stood for. The newspaper feature stories and photographs of the HipHopEMass that the priest posted in the parish hall felt like a pointed insult to the detractors while celebrated as a sign of evangelical success to supporters. Soon, every sermon and conversation was parsed for a hidden hip-hop agenda, both pro and con.

People were uncomfortable, with the rap, with the thugs, with the gays and lesbians, with the strange new faces. Bishop Roskam had received several of Paula's emails expressing her feelings about hip-hop.

"There has been rage directed at me, at hip-hop, at the church wardens for allowing hip-hop to exist," Poppa T remembers of the growing criticism. "People have always been uncomfortable with the radical love of Christ. It asks too much of us. But if the church doesn't show that love to the stranger and the outcast who will? The soul of hip-hop and the soul of the church are both at stake in this ministry."

Finally, the extreme step of a consultation with the bishop was called for. On a bright morning in July, little more than a year after the first hip-hop street mass was celebrated, Bishop Roskam once again came to the South Bronx. Only this time she did not come to join in welcoming the children of hip-hop but to help calm bitter emotions among the elders of Trinity.

That was the agenda as people took their seats beneath poster-sized photographs of various rectors, including Father Roberts and Poppa T, each standing proudly in front of Trinity surrounded by acolytes and other children newly confirmed in the faith.

⤳

About forty people filled the parish hall behind the sanctuary, and yet as people made their way to folding chairs the tension seemed to muffle conversation. The earlier meetings at Trinity about the HipHopEMass had been impassioned, but none carried the sense of showdown like this one.

It had begun civil enough. Bishop Roskam began by explaining the Christian Priority for Empathy, for trying to understand one another and assume the best in one another. She reminded people to speak for themselves, using "I" instead of "they," before going around the room, asking each person what their feelings were.

Poppa T sat at a table in front with the bishop and members of the vestry. Paula, who held no official church office, sat with them rather than with the others in the room. The priest was asked to just listen and if he felt compelled or was asked to respond, to do so as briefly as possible. The proceedings had

the feeling of a court trial with rap, the hip-hop ministry, and
Poppa T as the co-defendants. Before the meeting, back in the
rectory, he had held Jubilee and prayed. Entering the parish
hall, he exchanged a few perfunctory "hello's" and somber ac-
knowledgments with those parishioners who would meet his
eyes. It seemed as if everyone from Trinity Church was there.
He prayed again.

Taking his seat, he saw Glory and his father sitting with
the others. The teenage rapper smiled at him, and upon seeing
him there, Poppa T felt calmer, resolved "to let truth do its
work." Glory had been the first to be baptized through the
HipHopEMass. He saw Glory as a symbol of what all this was
for. He and others like him were why the priest was here.

≈

For almost four hours, through lunch and into the afternoon,
members of Trinity vented their anger, confusion, and fears
about the HipHopEMass in general and Poppa T and the rappers in particular. In protecting the core strengths and truths
of their faith as they understood them, Paula and other like-
minded church leaders prosecuted their case against hip-hop
culture. As musical director and vestry member Frank Poin-
dexter would say later, "How can children exposed to the evils
of rap — seeing people shot in radio stations, hearing such violent lyrics, the glorification of drugs — understand when we're
telling them to turn this into something for your God and savior, your Lord, your heavenly Christ? They're twelve-, eleven-,
ten-year-old kids and they are seeing something completely
different out in the street."

Trinity's traditions, Paula's supporters explained, were being
attacked by the prophetic vision of change called for by the
HipHopEMass. They objected to Trinity's rap ministry and its
growing reputation in the diocese and in the press as a hip-hop
church. They condemned what they saw as the irreverence of
the rappers in the pews and around the altar.

Some parishioners who wanted the ministry shut down claimed they weren't against rap but saw the hip-hop ministry as beside the point. They called the rappers Poppa T's "hobby" and "not really members of the church."

Some were angry. Others, the eldest, simply seemed hurt and puzzled. "You like them so much, Father Tim, but what about us?" they asked. "All we hear about is the children. We are aging. We just want a nice place to be buried."

The priest understood what they were saying. Rarely did any one under the age of fifty attend parish meetings. Hadn't he buried almost eighty elderly members of the congregation since arriving at Trinity, including Father Roberts? But he also couldn't help feeling that simply wanting a beautiful place to be buried was a very limited view of faith. Yes, of course, when you turn eighty or ninety, funerals are very much on people's mind, but he was sad when he thought how the parishioners had managed to finance most of a $175,000 renovation of the bricks and mortar but were hard-pressed to find the money to spread the Holy Spirit through hip-hop outreach, to speak to and for the thugs.

After all, he had come to Trinity with three clear objectives. Yes, one of them was to minister to an aging parish. But as he had done in Birmingham, he came to minister to and among children as well and to welcome more Hispanic churchgoers from the neighborhood. Yet when the children finally were invited to take part in the traditional service that one Sunday, they were made to feel unwelcome and, as this consultation with the bishop illustrated, all hell had broken loose. Not that anyone at Trinity was personally rude to the children, but hardly anyone went out of their way to be particularly friendly either.

So when a few aging members of the congregation spoke as if the neighborhood and the church were in conflict, two different communities with separate interests, he felt compelled to reply. "We're all one community here," he said, choosing his words carefully and suppressing his natural tendency to preach. "The community is the parish and the parish is the community. That means opening our doors to the neighborhood."

Bishop Roskam then turned to Marjorie Jones. Eloquent and elegant, with a graceful air that led the priest to affectionately dub her Lady Barrington, her resonant Jamaican accent underscored her point. "How many people here are under the age of fifty-five? Fifty? Forty?" She paused meaningfully. Only a few isolated hands remained in the air, including Sam's and Glory's.

Speaking stirringly in defense of the HipHopEMass, she explained that the new ministry did not threaten the beloved old traditions. The 11:00 a.m. Sunday service could stay 'high church,' keeping its incense and orthodoxy, while the HipHopEMass could make faith credible again for a previously unchurched generation. As diminished as Trinity's traditional membership was, she suggested, the new energy might even help sustain and support the aging congregation.

"I can't understand the upset over hip-hop," she concluded flashing her brilliant smile. "It's nothing but ministry to the patois."

The focus then turned from the priest to Mr. Warren and Lillas Bogle, a youthful seventy-one-year-old former nursing supervisor who was a descendant of Paul Bogle, the great Jamaican freedom fighter and Baptist deacon. As Trinity's wardens, they had steadfastly supported the hip-hop ministry before the vestry. Their goodwill and understanding had been crucial from the beginning. Now they were the target of some pointed criticism from people they had worshipped beside over many decades.

"It got raucous," Mr. Warren recalls. "People would get up and say hip-hop was negative and Tupac was a criminal. We read passages from his book, about who would help the thugs, who would speak for those with no voice. Father Tim said speaking for those with no voice is part of the ministry. But they'd say, 'The thugs? Who wants to speak for the thugs?'"

As the criticism became more personal and passions rose, Bishop Roskam again admonished the crowd to remember the Christian Priority for Empathy. Instead, the old Christian Predilection for Persecution seemed to be winning the day. The noise in the parish hall made Marjorie Jones frown and shake her head.

There were more objections to the language and the un-Christian values of gangsta rap that many feared had been unleashed into the church and condoned by the HipHopEMass. Sitting silently in his seat, Poppa T was not so sure that the vestry wouldn't benefit from listening to some gangsta rap. Let's not throw the baby out with the bath water, he thought. Ever since the gunshots coming from Forest Houses stopped, he had asked in every way he knew, 'Are we listening to our children and young people?' He didn't like the curse words or the hate. In fact, he never allowed it. Never. He had even turned away a DJ from Forest Houses whose mix was too raw. Yet despite the legitimate criticism, he could not help thinking there was great integrity in many raps containing curse words.

As parishioner after parishioner vented the same fears and anger, it was all he could do to stay sitting and keep his mouth shut. What he wanted to do was throw open the doors, point outside to the PJs only thirty feet away and tell them, "If we're really listening to the hearts and souls of those we profess to love — our young, our children — we had better know some of the rhyme and rap that is called gangster. There's some serious message going on." It didn't belong in his ministry or at the altar. But it was ground zero, the honest place to start.

Bishop Roskam began interrupting parishioners going on too long, repeating the same complaints or speaking disrespectfully. Paula was frustrated. She was getting the distinct impression this bishop wasn't at Trinity to consult and listen but to defend hip-hop even though it was the uncritical acceptance of hip-hop she believed was the problem.

Finally, Joe Barrett, the retired police detective formerly stationed in the notorious Bronx precinct known as Fort Apache, rose from his seat. When he began to speak, the room settled out of respect and his deep, measured tone calmed emotions. In the old days, the neighborhood children never tired of his two magic tricks, and he never tired of making his silk handkerchief float or of plucking a "bright idea" in the form of a tiny flashing red light from above some unsuspecting head. If anyone could bridge the divide, he could. He loved the children and was even godfather to three of DJ Old School Sam's kids.

"Father Holder, we need education in hip-hop," he offered. "We don't want to be the church that didn't welcome the children of the hip-hop generation. We don't want to be known as the church that made Father Holder choose between us and them."

It was clear not many others, however, were willing to learn, to compromise, or to welcome the children indoors. Things had become too polarized.

As the hours passed, Poppa T prayed mightily. He took a deep breath. Bishop Roskam gave him the opportunity to respond. "Rappers are the messengers of the day," he told Trinity. "God has sent these people to revitalize and rebuild this church and take it into a new day. We need to get out of the way. One of the things God is doing today is hip-hop."

✦

Finally Paula spoke. Poised and no nonsense, she began, "Father Tim doesn't know this but I like him." Paula began. "And I'm not going to hold your sexuality against you . . ."

The priest suppressed a smile. Paula always seemed to make a big point of not holding his sexuality against him. But she sure did hold it up at every opportunity.

Backed by family, friends of her late father, and traditional members of the congregation, the woman who had grown up literally within the walls of the church expressed love for Trinity and its traditions. She argued that those traditions exist for good and faithful reasons, that the liturgy of the Episcopal Church is worship, not entertainment.

Shifting on his metal folding chair, Poppa T understood her point. But he also realized that it was the church that needed to be elevated on this score, and it was hip-hop that could lead the way. A lot of folks in the Anglo-Catholic tradition, and at Trinity in particular, think it's all about the preciosity and the beauty of it all, the priest was thinking. On one hand, he agreed with Paula. Their tradition is about worshipping God with beauty and holiness, but most importantly, he believed, it is about the meaning of catholic as universal and whole. It is about the completeness of God's love and his embrace. And to be truly universal, to be truly a disciple of Jesus Christ, the most important question is "How did we love?" And not just how did we love our own but how did we love the stranger, here, today, on the corner of 166th Street and Trinity Avenue?

He listened as Paula mocked his embrace of the name Poppa T, accused him of serving his own interests instead of those of the church, and objected to how hip-hop brought into Trinity the very stereotypes that they as black people had fought so hard to escape. This was a clearing of the air and she did not hold back.

"Father Tim is a racist," she remembers saying. "By not taking into account the language and culture of hip-hop and how that perpetuates a society that keeps people down at a certain level is racist. Am I being clear?"

Marjorie Jones let out a small involuntary noise, somewhere between a gasp and a guffaw. Sam and Glory couldn't believe they heard correctly.

"If we're going to bring something into the church that is different, it should help youth express themselves in a way that they would be able to go out into any business and be successful," she said in making her argument. "Continuing to use hip-hop language that they already hear every single day is not going to help them. What we need is to meet the need in this community, to develop programs — job training, tutoring, senior programs — that would elevate them rather than keeping them at the same level. The fact of the matter is hip-hop keeps our youth in linguistic slavery. So yes, by Tim continuously pushing hip-hop, I feel that it is racist."

He had sat in contentious vestry meetings before. People had tried to use his sexuality to discredit him and the ministry before. He had gone through this sort of conflict — this pain — before. But just last March the majority of the vestry had supported him and voted to save the HipHopEMass at Trinity. And he was the rector of Trinity. He was doing his job.

Yes, he had heard all of this or some variation of it whispered or shouted by critics at some point in the past year. He was learning to just be quiet and listen — or at least he was trying to. He wasn't a saint. He understood what they were saying. He had made mistakes. He hadn't fully appreciated the depth of feeling over what he was asking of the longtime congregation. This ministry required everyone to grow in faith and understanding. It forced them all to look in mirrors. He was no exception. But Moses is dead, he thought. Get over it. Let the dead bury the dead.

"I didn't like what I heard at that meeting I attended," Sam explained later. "I didn't like the way they expressed their feelings. Everybody's pointing the finger, saying rap is wicked, saying it was a negative thing and not really welcomed. I was, like, let me fall back. I wouldn't DJ no more after that. Politics got involved."

At the time he wanted to speak up for Poppa T, but he knew better than to get involved. Just keep your head down, stay out of other people's fights. That was the way he had always lived, always survived. The church was more like the projects than these people were willing to admit.

Damn, he felt bad for the man. Poppa T had always been good to him. The priest had hired him as the sexton, at Trinity after he baptized him. Poppa T even bought him a suit for the occasion and agreed to be his godfather. With his first paycheck as sexton he gave the priest his first street bling, a shining, sparkling cross he wore with pride both on the street and over his cassock at highest altar. But what could he say? He didn't even know how to say it. If he spoke up, it would come out all wrong. All he knew is that when he was a kid living in Forest Houses, he didn't really know this church even existed, not in any meaningful sense. It was just there, with its own ways, its own people from outside the 'hood.

Sure, Trinity had the Caribbean festivals out on the street with great food but the 'hood ate and kept going. Poppa T embraced the whole neighborhood. He not only went outside but also invited everyone inside as well. He always told people, "Come inside, come visit the church."

As the hours and the anger mounted, Sam didn't want to hear anymore. He didn't understand all the ugliness. You just take the good with the bad, he thought. The HipHopEMass was a good thing. What was wrong with trying to mix the Christian life with rap since it's what a lot of kids listen to? He just didn't see anything wrong with it. The way these people were talking about hip-hop and Poppa T, now *that* he saw plenty wrong with.

"They took the fun out of it," Sam says. "When you hear people fighting, how the elder members didn't like it, how others did, I just figured to let this church live or go away on its own."

⌀

After Paula spoke and before Bishop Roskam adjourned the meeting, Glory raised his hand to speak. Everyone was exhausted. Emotions had been pitched high for almost four hours and the tension in the room weighed heavily. Until this moment, Trinity's old guard had dominated the meeting. Now someone from the hip-hop congregation was daring to speak. He hadn't planned to say anything, but he just had to talk, not to defend Poppa T or pick a side but to explain what hip-hop truly was and could be. He had to let them know he was there rapping for the Lord.

The crowd turned to the young man. Before saying a word, Glory smiled at Poppa T, and that is when the priest knew the ministry would last. It had roots. It would bear fruit in other seasons. He wasn't so sure about Trinity Church of Morrisania, however, or at least the Trinity so many in the parish hall had known and loved for so long. And then, like everyone else, he looked up to the young man in baggy pants and huge diamond earring and listened.

"I know I'm not going to college," Glory began quietly. "I'm a rapper. Before I discovered God, I was just looking to take the pain away. Growing up where I'm from, if you don't have a basketball or a dance group or you're not doing hip-hop, it's so easy to do the wrong thing like selling drugs. If you don't have something like that, the wrong thing is the easy thing."

He stopped, pausing so long some wondered if that was all he had to say. Finally, he raised his eyes and looked around the parish hall at the old faces watching him.

"Hip-hop is the weapon God gave me to fight the negativity in the 'hood," he resumed, his voice calm and steady. "We call it the 'hood 'cause it *is* the 'hood. Rap kept me away from the bad. I learned a lot from the street, about who I didn't want to be, but God working through rap pushed me in the right way."

His voice was gaining speed and confidence.

"I don't care if Poppa T is gay," he said, and the room became even more still. "That didn't stop the blessing. He blessed me. I'm here for God, and he's speaking to me in my language about how to be right in my relationship with God. That's my brother, don't matter the age, the skin color, the sexuality. Whatever Poppa T might be, who can judge? Everybody a born sinner. And we all children of God. All I know is this man's the only one talking to me. He's my priest. What Poppa T's doing and why I'll always have love and respect for him is he's going outside, going into the projects, handing out pamphlets. I'd go with him rapping about the Lord. We opened the doors and month after month the pews started filling up. You might say what we're doing is sin, is the devil, but I say it's our future."

The priest felt himself getting emotional. After hours of everyone criticizing rap as violent, dark, and evil, Glory, Son of the Bronx, was showing them as he never could what the ministry meant. A born and raised South Bronx rapper was opening the door to him, to them all. If the church could grasp what this young man was telling them about hip-hop's power to reach out, then the church had a chance of helping them heal and transcend their world. He felt he was watching the rise of a new Christian leader who understood that outside the walls and traditions of the church there were sons and daughters like him who spoke no other language.

"God gave me rap to love him, to talk to him, to pray to him," the young man continued softly. "I wouldn't be who I am without rap. And God wouldn't be who he is without my rap."

⤙⧢⤚

Glory sat down, and the silence lasted as his words settled among them. It was hard to interpret the quiet. Perhaps some of the people felt chastened or simply confused by this young man in oversized denim and earrings. But the priest was deeply moved by Glory's words. He knew he would remember this moment as one of the most important things to happen to him in his life.

Paula remembers asking, "Am I missing something? Is there something that I'm just not getting?" No one truly responded. But that night driving back to Brooklyn, she was glad to know that all this might be serving a good purpose. She was glad Glory had found Christ and was baptized through the hip-hop ministry.

Still, it was not the proper forum for Trinity. She did not want it in her church. People needed to respect and know the traditional Anglo-Catholic way of worship. And besides, it was manipulative of the priest to have invited the boy. The meeting was supposed to be only for the vestry and invited church members, like herself.

THE ROAD IS HOME

The priest made his way through the institutional echo of Bellevue Hospital to the prison ward where Adam was being held for psychiatric evaluation. He had meant to visit him sooner, but in the days following the shooting, he had instead gone door to door in the PJ tower with another member of Trinity introducing himself, asking how everyone was handling the aftermath, and inviting them to Trinity. But now the time seemed right. He wanted to speak with Adam. He needed to.

The headline of the press release from the Bronx district attorney's office read, "Grand Jury Charges Bronx Man with the Attempted Murder of Six Police Officers, Kidnapping and Other Offenses During Standoff in His Grandmother's Apartment." The official charges were six counts of attempted murder in the first degree, six counts of attempted murder in the second degree, three counts of kidnapping in the second degree, three counts of unlawful imprisonment in the first degree, three counts each of criminal possession of a weapon in the second and third degrees, and one count of reckless endangerment.

Adam faced up to twenty-five years to life imprisonment on each of the attempted murder charges and twenty-five years on each of the kidnapping charges. That's too many lifetimes to lose, Poppa T thought.

During the standoff, Adam had fired repeatedly at the police inside Forest Houses. He was being held without bail, just one more thug who deserved to be locked up and forgotten for a very long time. That's what anyone would think seeing the local newscasts or reading the *Post* or the *Daily News* accounts. That's what the grand jury indictment and a record of nine previous arrests seemed to prove.

But seven or eight people on Trinity Avenue and in Forest Houses, including Sam, didn't think so. That wasn't the Adam they knew. He just wasn't someone who would walk around carrying a gun and shooting or hurting people. It wasn't in his nature. That's what Sam said: It wasn't in his nature.

As the newspapers had reported, things began with a fight between father and son. The two had never got along, and Adam's father, who was absent more often than not from the young man's life, had started throwing things at him. He was angry that Adam had taken his grandmother out of the nursing home where he had put her and brought her back home to Forest Houses.

As Adam and his grandmother both separately confided in the priest, she had been put into the nursing home "*wayyyy* before she was ready or needed to go.*"* Adam had been incarcerated at the time his father forced "the only person who loved him" to leave her home, and he could do nothing to stop it. But as soon as he got out, he went to get her and bring her home.

That's when things went terribly wrong. According to the district attorney's office, Adam held his father and two health care workers hostage in his wheelchair-bound grandmother's apartment. Having overheard the hostage negotiators talking about her, the priest understood Adam's grandmother was also in the apartment throughout the siege.

As the early morning fight turned loud and physical, Adam became confused, upset, and overwhelmed. He lashed out. He thought he was protecting his grandmother. He believed he was helping her, saving her. He was just trying to bring her home.

That's what made him "go against his nature" and hold his own family and 'hood at gunpoint.

Poppa T wasn't so sure Adam's was an uncommon story. A life of petty crime, broken relationships, parental abandonment, poverty, all the conditions that too often passed for normal in Forest Houses and PJs across the country. The thug life.

He wasn't a sociologist or a psychiatrist or a judge. He was a priest. A hip-hop priest. And as he waited to speak with Adam the Word of God and the words of Tupac gave him heart. He remembered the lines from Tupac's poem "Things That Make Hearts Break":

> *lonely children*
> *unanswered cries*
> *and souls who have given up hoping. . . .*

Adam was a child of God. The priest would not diminish or glorify his crimes, but he would listen to his story. And then he would share with the prisoner a better one, the story of God's redeeming love. It was God who could answer his cry and offer new hope.

After speaking with Adam's grandmother, hearing how he had rescued her from that place she was forced into and how grateful she was when he brought her home, Poppa T couldn't help believing there was a strain of good in this story — in Adam — that needed to be told.

Their meeting was private, between a man and his priest, but Adam seemed glad he had come. Before leaving, Poppa T let him know that much good had come from that terrible day. A ministry had been born. A church was awakened. "The Word was made flesh and dwelt in the 'Hood."

❧

Poppa T left Adam and Bellevue with his purpose and resolve to continue the HipHopEMass strengthened. In fact, he started to think now was the time to take it on the road full-time. If

Trinity Church in the holy land of hip-hop did not want the HipHopEMass crew, then, like Jesus told his disciples, they would stomp the dust from their feet and go to where they would be heard.

Let others argue endlessly over the nature of hip-hop. It was the nature of God he now needed to focus on. He would stop defending hip-hop just as he had stopped defending his sexuality back in Alabama or, years earlier, his faith in God to his sophisticated secular friends in politics. Oh sure, he would have to explain the ministry to the naysayers and the uninformed, but he would never again apologize for hip-hop.

It was time to stop fighting the negative stereotypes and reputation and instead commit fully to living and preaching the best of what this ministry stood for at both altar and street. As Bishop Roskam had said when Paula and the others pointed only to the worst in rap and the evils of the streets, "Let's not forget about the goodness of the streets."

Arguing with people who couldn't or wouldn't understand only kept them from reaching those who were hungry to hear the Word. All they needed to do was ask God in all vernaculars, tongues, and cultures for leadership, courage, and vision, he decided. The messengers might be imperfect but the message was not. They would continue to worship and celebrate God creatively, positively, and ecumenically with and for everyone. Let those with ears listen.

He was done fighting. Or rather, standing with D-Cross, Jahneen, Glory, and the others, he would go on fighting for souls, but he was done fighting for approval. The rest was in God's hands.

He loved Trinity and the South Bronx. He had friends here now and a calling. "I'll be here until I have a hip-hop heart attack or a hip-hop kick in the pants out of here," he would laugh only half-jokingly to those who asked about the future of the rap ministry and his future at Trinity. Both seemed a distinct possibility in light of the implacable campaign being waged against hip-hop within the church and his own penchant for the deep-fried.

⧼⧽

Like a wildstyle graffiti mural that covers the entire side of a subway car, the hip-hop church movement is an unlikely work of audacity and incursion. It insists and imagines, disrespects boundaries and adds lots of color. Perhaps most importantly, it is a declaration of purpose and identity for those to whom both are denied, an expression of those too long ignored. The graffiti artists who in the 1970s transformed the New York subway fleet into an electrified, high-speed laboratory for art and style were criminalized, just as today's hip-hop worshippers are accused of defacing what the church is and stands for.

The HipHopEMass is only one style of Christian worship, one shade of Episcopalian in a larger spectrum and, like graffiti on a subway car, often misunderstood or only partially seen as it hurtles past, a flash of color or an impression too bright and too bold to be easily read. But the impression for most is quick and strong: it is the work of vandals.

⧼⧽

On All Saints' Day in November 2005, D-Cross the Living Instrument and D.O. stalk the crowd filling Trinity's pews and call out "God is great!" and the people respond "Alla the time!"

As always, the service adheres to the Book of Common Prayer, but the music and lexicon are hip-hop. The five elements of hip-hop — DJing, MCing, breakdancing, graffiti, and cultural style — have been amended or added to by every social commentator or hip-hop visionary who has ever wielded an issue of *Vibe*, but it's never been questioned that it's "style" that unites the elements and elevates them from individual disciplines to a cultural force. And style is why ministries like the HipHopEMass are so controversial.

Style, it has been written, was a way for early rappers, breakdancers, and graffiti artists to defy a hostile world. In it they found a way to generate something from nothing. Today hip-hop defies a hostile church. Breakdancing in the nave, rapping the Lord's Prayer, giving a backbeat to the Eucharist are all acts of defiance, not of what the church stands for but of the ways it has failed itself and fallen short. Faith without deeds, as the scripture says, is worthless. Hip-hop style, in this case, demands substance. It generates something from nothing.

Trinity, like other communities, didn't become hostile to the children of hip-hop when they first swaggered in the front door. They ignored and feared them long before that. But the children came anyway, bringing their rap and their style, saying, "Look at me." They defied those who judged them to look away, to pretend they didn't see. They may not have liked what they saw, but the church could not be blind to them any longer.

And the church was not. At the All Saints service that night, Archdeacon Faga Tuatagaloa-Matalavea from Samoa, representing 75 million Anglicans at the United Nations, walked beside Poppa T, D-Cross, D.O., and the Forest Houses children in the opening processional as Jahneen and the EMass band performed Kanye West's "Jesus Walks." Among them was Reverend Lyndon Harris, whose church stands at ground zero, across from where the World Trade Towers fell, and who on 9/11 opened St. Paul's doors to all needing shelter of any kind and has not closed them since. He stood behind the altar with Poppa T rocking side to side while D-Cross and D.O. freestyled.

And the city was not blind to them any longer, either. Democratic Party mayoral candidate and Bronx native Freddy Ferrer entered Trinity with his wife and small entourage on the eve of the election he would lose. Perhaps it was coincidental, but the candidate did not enter until after Jahneen finished reading from Ecclesiastes: "Let us sing the praises of famous men and women. . . ."

Standing before the altar, D-Cross rapped a simple prayer: "May God bless our city / Bless prisoners and those in pain / Bless bless y'all / Bless bless y'all. . . . " Then the archdeacon stepped forward, resplendent in her blue satin cape with gold embroidered crest, straw hat, and long white dress with a high-collared ruffle. She looked like a nineteenth-century island monarch. Her bearing combined the elegance and dignity of high church with the warmth and charisma of Samoa, and when she spoke, it was with the same voice that has the ear of the archbishop of Canterbury and world leaders.

She began her sermon noting that as Anglican observer at the U.N., her office represents all thirty-eight provinces of the Anglican Communion, "although not all are talking to each other." Quickly, however, she turned to the congregation and issue at hand. "We in the church," she read from a prepared text, "have always taken popular music and made it sacred by bringing it into the church. And why not?"

"Word," several voices responded.

Her sermon was about the importance of music to the church, about "making a joyful noise to the Lord" and "relaying the message of the Lord as faithfully as we can." While she did not know it, her embrace of popular music was the worst-case scenario for many at Trinity who were not in the pews this night. For them, the old beer hall tunes that fill Trinity's hymnals, retrofitted with pious lyrics, have been around long enough to shed their worldly origins. As the cliché goes, respectability, musical or otherwise, comes with age.

Finally, the archdeacon turned to the rappers and their style of praise.

"You have brought the world into your church through music," she concluded. "Now you just have to sing louder so your joyful noise is louder than the world."

"This year — 2006 — is our year of living on the road!" Poppa T shouted from any available rooftop. Around that time it was not uncommon for those on his email list to receive four, five, even six emails a day about all things hip-hop. Sometimes they were links to news accounts of the ministry's travels and travails or how one more rapper or preacher was joining Reverend Run, Mase, or Nas in the rising hip-hop church movement, announced with multiple exclamation points and bold-faced capital letters. The priest was not shy about electronic flaming.

He was constantly giving "Big ups!" to everyone from the EMass rappers putting together a Hip Hop Prayer Book to Katherine Jefferts Schori, the first woman elected head of the Episcopal Church, to Kanye West for speaking out against homophobia in hip-hop. Almost as often he was bringing to attention those rappers affiliated with Holy Hip Hop who preached a different gospel, including the L.A.-based IDOL King whose rap "Hope" spoke directly to clergy like him:

> *Now people are actually convinced*
> *these so-called gay pastors*
> *are really making sense*
> *and have good arguments*
> *Well I hate to drop a bomb*
> *A gay pastor's an oxymoron*

It got to the point that Jahneen, D-Cross, and others receiving Poppa T's upper-case e-shouts couldn't keep up. Poppa T was enthusiastic if he was anything. He worked tirelessly, his emails often sent late at night or in the predawn hours. Then one day among the cyber-blizzard of the priest's emails, one arrived with a subject line that stood out: "HipHopEMass.org 2006 PLANNING CALENDAR YES! YES! Y'ALL! 2006 Is Our Breakthrough Year! PRAY AND GIVE FOR HipHopEMass a Home in 2006! All love, Poppa T"

The calendar in the body of the email listed the revised schedule for monthly First Friday HipHopEMass services at Trinity, down from what had been weekly Sunday evening services in the beginning. But it also listed HipHopEMass services in prisons and churches in Ohio, Maryland, New Jersey, Texas, and Mississippi. And then something else: The Easter Resurrection Tour. Poppa T's prediction was coming true. This was

the year the hip-hop ministry would live — and find new life —
on the road.

The HipHopEMass crew is over three hours late leaving the
South Bronx. It's almost noon and Jahneen, D-Cross, D.O.,
down from Toronto, Poppa T, and the band are still loading
mike stands, speakers, Hip Hop Prayer Books, vestments, and
luggage into two cramped vans. The itinerary includes daily
services on street corners and in churches, correctional facilities, gymnasiums, and community halls throughout North
Carolina and Virginia.

Finally, the last extension cord and candy bar are packed.
Everyone is eager to hit the road, but before Poppa T will climb
into the passenger seat, he insists they follow him around the
corner. Standing in the middle of Trinity Avenue on the exact
spot where the first hip-hop service began with a prayer beneath the street-cathedral spires of the PJs, the priest invites
the hip-hop disciples to join hands.

As a few cars whiz by blaring rap, Jahneen reads the Easter
and Resurrection passages from Matthew 28:1–10: " . . . but the
angel said to the women, 'Do not be afraid; I know you are
looking for Jesus who was crucified. . . . Go quickly and tell his
disciples, "He has been raised from the dead." ' " Some young
men passing in an old Cadillac El Dorado slow down and
stare. "Suddenly Jesus met them and said, 'Greetings!' And
they came to him, took hold of his feet, and worshipped him."
One or two among the small number of friends and clergy
who have come to see them off seem self-conscious praying in
the street, but the HipHopEMass crew is unfazed. "Then Jesus
said to them, 'Do not be afraid; go and tell my brothers to go
to Galilee; there they will see me.' "

Finished, she closes the Bible and Poppa T offers a surprisingly brief prayer, perhaps conscious of the traffic and long road
ahead. But before they leave their circle and pile into the vans,
D.O. steps front and center and starts rapping. "Christ is back!"

Got me excited, feelin so eager...
Christ has risen, today on Easter
Saw the vision, stayed on the mission
Best believe, Christ is risen...

Spread the word out, there's no doubt...
CHRIST IS BACK!
Alleluia, couldn't have come sooner
CHRIST IS BACK!

Kurtis was back. He didn't caravan with the others from the South Bronx. Instead, he would be driving the white Mercedes from Harlem, meeting up with everyone in North Carolina, but he was back.

After Kurtis left the HipHopEMass to start his own Hip Hop Church America ministry, Poppa T and Kurtis did not speak for quite some time. The rapper's confirmation and ordination studies ended as suddenly as they had begun. At first the priest was confused by this change of heart, but when he learned Kurtis was starting the Hip Hop Church in Harlem, with the support of more theologically conservative ministers, he could not help thinking Kurtis had become uneasy with the Episcopal Church's "left-leaning" reading of scripture, particularly concerning homosexuality.

The HipHopEMass was a "come as you are" ministry and emphasized acceptance of all. "We don't mix holy scripture with misogyny or homophobia," Poppa T once said, making the distinction between the HipHopEMass and Holy Hip Hop. "We're using the language and loops to build people up, not tear them down."

In countless discussions about the peace, love, and unity of hip-hop and of their ministry, the priest claims he never saw the King of Rap's departure coming. When he first heard the terse voicemail in which Kurtis resigned, he was afraid the new ministry wouldn't survive without him. But it did survive. In fact, it even grew. And so had the Hip Hop Church America ministry Kurtis was leading. The hip-hop church movement was making inroads into virtually every Christian denomination.

As time went by and Kurtis studied theology and prepared to become an ordained pastor, his Hip Hop Church became strongly ecumenical. In rapid order Kurtis founded hip-hop congregations in Lutheran, Baptist, Pentecostal, and A.M.E. churches from Harlem to Los Angeles. One of the reasons he had left the HipHopEMass, he explained more than a year after resigning as musical director, was "because I didn't want to be trapped under the confines of the Episcopalian doctrine. I'm nondenominational. I believe that Jesus wanted all of us to come together and praise God, no age limit, no sex, no race, no denomination."

From the earliest days, both men agreed on certain goals for the ministry, that it would "sing the new song of Jesus Christ in the vernacular — the language of the people — especially our younger generations; to celebrate the roots of hip-hop as evangelists for his love — spiritually, pastorally, socially, and politically — at street and altar; to serve the poor, the sick, and those in prison; and to serve as a model bringing together other faith communities as well as welcoming those with no faith from throughout the city and nation." However, some of the other goals that emerged, including "raising up leaders for the church — hip-hop priests, deacons, and laity," struck Kurtis as more sectarian than made him comfortable.

Back when Poppa T and Kurtis first talked over *hamburguesas con queso* and Cokes and were thinking of a new name for their ministry, the priest was adamant about calling it the HipHopEMass. Kurtis liked the priest's line that the E stood for Everybody, but it also began to feel as if it increasingly stood for Episcopalian. He had wanted to call what they were creating the Hip Hop Church. "It's a better name," he laughingly confides. "More commercial."

Today both ministries, both names, were part of the promise of the rising hip-hop church movement. And in the spirit of Kurtis's Hip Hop Church — "Anybody can have it, just like anybody can have Jesus wherever they are" — the old differences, whether over doctrine or sexuality, no longer seemed so insurmountable. "We're all in this thing together," Kurtis came to believe. "Everyone is equal under God." He was ready to embrace the Episcopalians again.

Kurtis made the first overture a few months earlier, inviting Poppa T and some members of the HipHopEMass crew to Harlem. He introduced the priest as the man who brought him into the church. Poppa T responded by thanking Kurtis for being the man who brought him into hip-hop.

When planning the Resurrection Tour, Kurtis was one of the first people Poppa T invited to be part of the traveling posse. Again, Kurtis did not hesitate to accept.

AT STREET AND ALTAR

The Remnant drove through the night from Atlanta to appear with the HipHopEMass in Chapel Hill, North Carolina, the first stop of what Poppa T had billed the Easter Resurrection Tour. D-Cross and Jahneen headed down Interstate 95 in separate vans, the Living Instrument riding with four members of the most recent line-up of the EMass band as well as Crystal Agapé. The young female rapper from California was joining the HipHopEMass for the first time, and initially her gentle manner and delicate frame made everyone think of her as a shy kid sister. But soon they would see her fierce intensity when spitting rhymes or talking God.

Jahneen, accustomed to touring in far greater comfort with headliners like Grover Washington and Kool and the Gang, crammed without complaint into a rental van with five others, including Poppa T and D.O. After meeting Kurtis, Jahneen, and Poppa T in October 2004 at the World Council of Churches conference in Atlanta, D.O. had begun making frequent trips down to Trinity from Toronto and quickly had become an integral part of the HipHopEMass crew. Now, armed with dozens of copies of his new CD and a wardrobe of oversized basketball jerseys of seemingly every college team along the Resurrection Tour itinerary, the soft-spoken rapper sat quietly in the way-back, a big grin on his face across three states.

As the van crossed the Mason-Dixon line into the South Poppa T began waxing poetic about the joys of Southern cooking and anticipating his return to a beloved chain restaurant heavy on the gravy. Jahneen, ever the pro, slept. Everyone else was too excited.

⌘

The Church of the Holy Family, in an affluent, white neighborhood on a street beneath a canopy of large trees, is a far cry from the concrete and razor wire of the South Bronx. This evening the church is packed with adults, children, and teenagers, many who have traveled from nearby towns and different churches.

High school senior Justin Mortell, eighteen, wasn't going to come, but he was asked to work as "quote unquote security" even though he doesn't think they need that in Chapel Hill. Several of his friends have been posting information about the HipHopEMass on their *myspace.com* pages for the past week and went to all kinds of churches around town to promote it. Their efforts have been successful. It looks as if it's going to be standing room only in the large, modern sanctuary.

"My parents hate rap music," Justin says, dragging more chairs out of the parish hall for the overflow. "They listen to Beatles or whatever. But this is for our generation. We grew up with hip-hop. It influenced the way we are." He "highly doubts" that his friends and the other teenagers in Chapel Hill took the time to learn much about the history of rap or the conditions in which it was born or now exists beyond listening to the music. Still, he thinks the HipHopEMass might open some eyes. Maybe beyond the beat they will hear the message. The message, he thinks, is simple: "I — any of us — could be" a thug.

A slew of kids from the Adam & Eve Dance Ministry in Haw River, a town thirty minutes away, arrive dressed in crisp khaki's and blinding white T-shirts and tennis shoes. Tony White, a slight African American man with a muscled dancer's body, created the nondenominational ministry with children from several different churches and dance studios, ranging from preschoolers to older teenagers. With very few exceptions, they are the only black faces in the suburban crowd. They were just going to come to watch, just to see what this hip-hop service was all about, but Poppa T asked them to join in the processional.

As the first blast of "Jesus Walks" from the EMass band fills the soaring vault, the Adam & Eve Dancers freestyle into the sanctuary, their exuberance carrying along the priests, rappers, and acolytes who lead the way holding aloft a golden crucifix and swinging incense burners.

Standing before the altar acting as MC, D-Cross shouts, "Is God in the house?" and the crowd roars, "Yeah!"

The Living Instrument moves his heavy frame across the floor in what seems like one giant stride, arms and dreads swinging as he beatboxes, scratches, and cuts. "God is in the house!"

This is high hip-hop church and as the procession moves through the aisles, snaking around the entire sanctuary, some of the children and young people look at each other with huge smiles as if they can't believe this is happening in a church. As the crowd rises to its feet, a few older people exchange not quite such ecstatic glances as well.

Adam Beane of the Remnant, carrying the prayer book high above his dreadlocked head, leads the procession, surrounded by acolytes and clergy vested in full Episcopalian glory and clouds of incense. As he turns down the center aisle, making his way toward the altar, the crowd gets a good look at him sporting a large T-shirt that reads, "Religion Kills, Jesus Lives."

Justin breaks into a little smile. Nothing like this has ever happened in his church — or Chapel Hill — before.

❧

"The HipHopEMass is cool because it removes blinders to both Christ's love and hip-hop," Adam offers the following morning in a motel breakfast room, his provocative T-shirt wadded in a ball on the floor in the Remnant's room upstairs.

"I'd never been in an Episcopal church," adds Niles Gray, the quiet one of the group who has a way with the devastating one-liner. "But I believe in Jesus so whatever."

Adam looks at Niles for a beat in mock pity. "You mean 'I believe in Jesus and *something*,'" Adam corrects him.

Just-John ostentatiously ignores them both. "Both the clubs where we appear and now the EMass are often smokin'."

"I came to hip-hop after listening to Snoop's 'Doggy Style,'" Niles remembers happily, in his own world. Then his face droops. "Mom put me on punishment."

"He's still on punishment," Just-John deadpans.

"As it should be," Adam adds sternly.

Niles, now morose, hangs his head. "As it should be...."

The seamless banter sounds glib. The Remnant and their love of God and hip-hop do not. The three "rap disciples" know hip-hop is under attack for its raw language, sexism, homophobia, and the gangsta life it glamorizes. That's where gospel rap, Holy Hip Hop, Christian rap, or whatever the music industry is calling it this week, comes in. Rap can be a powerful force for good if it can avoid the pitfalls of the marketplace. "What's catchy today is tomorrow's parody if it's not coming from a real place," Just-John warns.

"We're optimistic," says Adam. "You can say 'Jesus' on the radio now. It's not a black hole. Serious rap artists are putting that one gospel track on their CDs. But hip-hop hasn't evolved enough. Gangsta rap has been dominant for ten years. And people can mock and manipulate even the gospel for profit."

"But more rappers are stepping out, speaking what God put on their mind," says Just-John.

Adam and Just-John turn to Niles, to see what he has to say. He seems taken unaware. "What?" he says defensively. "I'm on punishment."

Julio Herrera found Romans 10 while he was still a crack addict. He's talking about the verse that goes, "I have been found by those who did not seek me; I have shown myself to those who did not ask for me."

At the time his career was over, his house empty of furniture, and the utilities were cut off. Since then, he had gone through some hard times, but he had found and was following God now. Or at least trying hard to. And, like everything else important that happened to him, good and bad, he would put it to music.

He wrote the song, the one about that other life he had lived, the one that nearly killed him, on a Monday. On Wednesday he had the gig.

After Kurtis resigned as musical director, Poppa T, not wanting to miss a beat, immediately began searching for a replacement, and Jahneen again came through, having worked in the studio and on the road with Julio over the years. He says this kicking back in the van carrying the musicians to Charlotte, the next stop on the tour, while the old R&B musicians and the rappers argue good-naturedly in the back seats.

"Jesus still taboo on radio," laments D-Cross, shaking his massive dreads. "It's violence makes money."

Several voices rise above the sound of the highway, but when bassist David Burnett, who they affectionately call the Godfather of the HipHopEMass, starts to speak, everyone shuts up. It's clear the older man has their respect and not just because his bass lines have been sampled on countless tracks from 50 Cent to Fantasia.

"Ludacris charges," he says softly in his smooth baritone. "We give it away."

The musicians bust out laughing. The entire band makes only $650 for each hip-hop service. They have been living on pennies and a prayer. But the Godfather isn't finished, and they are silent again when he claims, "God-centered rap can make money, too."

There's a rumbling of skepticism. "It's got the right message," the Godfather responds. "Eighty percent of black males between sixteen and thirty are goin' to jail. This rap is important because it's a way to do something about these statistics.

These are the children of Martin Luther King, Malcolm X, George Washington Carver. They have every right to hear a message of hope."

There is an appropriate moment of silence while this sinks in, then the yelling starts all over again on a new topic.

"Listen, 'Jesus Walks' was the first — "

"That weren't the first — "

"Hammer was among the first gospel rappers out there," insists D-Cross. "Listen to 'Holy Ghost Boy.' "

"No, listen to Pigeon John!" someone yells.

"That ain't God rap!"

"It's no 'Swing Low Sweet Chariot,' but that talent come from God!"

"The fact is — "

"Lemme finish!"

"It was Steve Wiley back in the '80s who did the first Christian rap — "

"You trippin'?"

"Just listen to — "

"Now why would I wanna go and do *that?*"

❧

On the road by 5:00 a.m., they have a long drive ahead. Last night in Charlotte the HipHopEMass disciples closed down Mert's Heart & Soul Food. Or rather, opened it up. The place was about to lock up, but when the head cook found out Kurtis Blow was hungry, tables were pushed together and paper napkins, clean forks, and menus materialized.

The crew had the whole place to themselves. The laughter, the good-natured ribbing, and rehashing of old stories felt like a family reunion. Poppa T was talking to everyone. Sitting in the center of the long table, Kurtis smiled and was quiet, seeming to take in all the new faces and how many miles he had come, how far they all had come. Before, during, and after the fried chicken, pork chops, greens, macaroni and cheese, and sweet potato pie, every busboy, cook, manager, and waiter in the place got a picture taken with the King of Rap.

Beneath record sleeves of old 45s and LPs hanging on the walls like religious icons, Poppa T made a toast welcoming Kurtis back home to the ministry he helped get off the ground. Aretha, Sam, B.B., and the faces of countless other musical legends and saints looked down on the gathering.

It was late when the party finally broke up and everyone wandered their own way into the sultry Charlotte night.

Now this morning, the only sound inside the vans is the hum of the highway. When the little caravan, minus Kurtis driving the white Mercedes to the next tour stop, pulls over at a service station to gas up, it's not quite yet fully daylight. Everyone stumbles glassy-eyed with fatigue into the overlit convenience store. Breakfast is a buffet of candy, chips, and vending machine coffee. Jahneen and Julio buy souvenirs of North Carolina — a fridge magnet, a shot glass — a tradition for the tour veterans, a way to commemorate one more stretch of the road.

⋐⋙

D-Cross and D.O., whose freestyle immediacy usually ignites the crowds, take the stage in a church parking lot at the corner of Main and Dillard, a blighted intersection in central Durham. The congregation of St. Philip's is here in numbers but, like Trinity, they are a commuter congregation. Mostly white and older, they worship but do not live in this mostly black and impoverished corner of the city. They are trying to join those who do. So far, the curious from the neighboring retirement home, homeless shelter, and housing blocks are lingering at a safe distance

"Y'all ready for church?" D.O. shouts into the mike. The day is too hot and bright and the weather has made the crowd listless.

"Say yes yes, y'all! Say bless bless, y'all!" His baby blue University of North Carolina basketball jersey streaks back and forth as he works the crowd.

"Spread the word, there is no doubt," he starts rapping, "Christ is back!"

He holds out the microphone. "Christ is back!" a few scattered voices respond.

"Alleluia, couldn't have come sooner!" D.O. again points the mike at the crowd.

"Christ is back!" call a few more voices this time.

The HipHopEMass band helps get the crowd clapping as D.O. stalks across the broken asphalt. Kurtis is scratching at his silver turntable, and the crowd inches closer.

Couldn't express the feeling I was looking for the words
My man on the block came up and said "Word!"
Tossin' and turnin' like I couldn't sleep
And when I woke up, looked up to see
Workin' so hard tryin' to live my dreams
Martin Luther King, said he had a dream
All had to do was think it, cause if I speak it,
I can be it . . . and live all my dreams
The word was flesh and dwelt in the 'hood
And when the sun rose it was all understood
I was lookin' all over, couldn't find a clue
'Til I realized, it's in me, it's in you

Said I was lookin' all over, searchin' for the truth
'Til I realized, it's in me, it's in you

The word was flesh and dwelt in the 'hood
And when the sun rose it was all understood

The word was flesh and dwelt in the 'hood
And when the sun rose it was all understood

When D-Cross joins in beatboxing behind D.O.'s rap, two men in stained sweatshirts and baggy pants, one young, one considerably older, start to dance wildly in front of the crew. Drunk, or high, they threaten to upstage the rappers and when the older man starts to crowd Julio at the keyboard, some church people in the crowd look as if they think this might not have been such a great idea after all.

Then Julio laughs and D-Cross takes the guy's hand, bumps shoulders with him in a half-embrace. "I gave the guy a pound and said, 'God bless,'" he tells everyone in the van later. "He said, 'I'm enjoying the service.' His exact words. He knew he was in church."

As the man dances away from the band, shouting, "Alleluia!" about a dozen other homeless men and women watch from the corner across the street where drug deals happen. Mixing up front with the church crowd from St. Philip's are about twenty of the Adam & Eve Dancers who have followed the HipHopEMass from the service in Chapel Hill. As they step and "liturgical breakdance" through the steaming parking lot and along the broken sidewalks, their joy and energy or maybe just the unlikely spectacle draw in more of the locals and transients watching from a distance.

There are even some teenagers who heard about the Resurrection Tour and drove forty miles because, in the words of one young man, "it ain't often something like this happens, a hip-hop service."

"My mom told me," says Nicholas, nineteen, dressed in black from Nikes to skullcap, a yellow "LIVESTRONG" bracelet the only flash of color. "It sounded different so why not come down?"

"I love most hip-hop," interrupts his neatly cornrowed brother Steffan, seventeen. "People love hip-hop as long as it's hip-hop."

Nicholas starts to say that he has heard Christian rappers before and is trying to remember some names, when his brother's friend Ross, sixteen, interrupts to say, "I would listen to Christian rap if it was good."

The young men exchange meaningful looks before they decide that so far today the rap has been "pretty good, not bad." But then they stop talking and crane their necks to see what is going on. The music has stopped.

The Remnant is up and they have started with "The Prayer," a powerful, music-free, prayer-rap in three individual sections. The crowd is mesmerized by Just-John, followed by Niles. As Adam recites his part, the older homeless man is still dancing with his bottle in a brown paper bag.

> *It's me again, pleading needing a fixing for my spiritual*
> *   addiction*
> *I pray to stay under your jurisdiction*
> *Holy and prudent*
> *See I commit the same sins over and over again and I'm*
> *   beginning*
> *To think I'm a nuisance; parts of my heart are dark*
> *But I'm still translucent. . . .*

The rapper looks at the man, looks at the crowd, and in a voice thick with emotion, he alters the words of the prayer to indicate everyone present:

> *So many wrong things I've done,*
> *Every girl whom after I lusted*
> *Each time I spoke a false tongue*
> *Or when my anger erupted into hysterical altercations*
> *I'd even try to offer you ultimatums like "If I go to church*
> *   on Sunday . . .*

. . . and here Adam turns his face to the dancing man the crowd is eyeing warily . . .

> *" . . . can I still hate him on Monday?"*

There is an audible intake of breath, an uncomfortable shift. They know the answer.

Durham is different from Chapel Hill, or Charlotte, or other stops so far on the Resurrection Tour. Elsewhere, the

HipHopEMass was treated like a concert by middle-class teenagers and like a curiosity by local newspapers. Here the hip-hop
disciples have come to those who, like Julio when he was on
crack, were not seeking God and who did not ask for him.

Just before the sacrament, after Kurtis has preached and the
rappers have rapped, Poppa T, wearing his white vestments,
takes the microphone. Several people are already moving in
the direction of the food tables. They came for hip-hop and
free barbeque. Besides, they have been standing on the asphalt
for almost two hours, and it's hot.

"God is in the street and at the altar," his voice cries from
the enormous speakers. "If the two are separated, we all die."
People are milling about, but the priest continues. "Hip-hop
is crying out, not dirty words but the words of Jeremiah,
Chronicles, the words of Mary Magdelene, of Jesus!"

There is a smattering of applause. "They called him a criminal. Well, the criminal Tupac stood up for our children too,
when the church did not. Today we do too!"

The exodus to the food table has slowed. The crowd is listening again. "God doesn't care about black or white, male or
female, gay or straight. We're talking about a God who loves it
all, made it all, watches over it all!"

The applause is huge. Even people in line for chicken and
potato salad applaud.

"Let us pray," says the priest, raising his arms high. "God,
bless all faiths and traditions. We know you are bigger than
any of them. We know you are in the surprise. You are joining
together the street and the altar, and for that we are grateful
because we need each other. You are the giver of life and you
have given us hip-hop to praise you. Amen. Word."

The line for barbeque snakes around the grassy patch where drug deals used to take place. A dozen members of a Carolina Football Development League team arrive too late for the music. The league uses football as a tool to teach life skills, academics, personal growth, and Christ. On the back of their Durham Raiders T-shirts are the words "1 Love, 1 Family, Be Safe."

Steve Jones, twenty-two, saw the HipHopEMass flyer, and since he had never heard of Christian hip-hop, he gave it to the coach. His teammate, Mike Tuten, twenty-two, the one they call Sleep, also got a flyer just that morning while the team was working on a house for Habitat for Humanity. Some of the players took off from the construction site, but the rest came because they heard it would be a strong fellowship and they are "a Christ-based team." One of the guys flexed his Jesus tattoo on his shoulder to underscore the point.

An African American woman is flipping through the Hip Hop Prayer Book being offered at a nearby folding table. "You changed God's word to hip-hop?" Her voice is pitched high to register her shock. "I don't agree with that. Uh-uh."

The young man behind the table selling Resurrection Tour T-shirts and handing out free copies of the Hip Hop Prayer Book says nothing. Also noncommittal, a few parishioners from St. Philip's and neighborhood teenagers finger the merchandise.

"Hip-hop is not a lifestyle," she says loudly to no one in particular. The people around the table are quiet. "It's a religion, and you shouldn't be mixing religions." She takes a free copy of the prayer book and stuffs it indignantly into her large canvas bag as she walks away.

There is an awkward silence until Allison, fifteen, one of the Adam & Eve dancers standing nearby, shrugs. "It's fun. It was worth the drive to watch the homeless guys dancing."

When her friend and fellow dancer Jasmine, sixteen, is asked what she thinks is the rappers' message, she replies instantly, "Thanking God."

Back in the van, driving across the state after a long day, D-Cross put it differently. "This drunk old dude is what it's all about," he said in that calm way of his that still somehow manages to convey passion. "I could feel the vibration of the people thinking, 'Ooh, this is about to go wrong.' But those guys were feeling it." He smiles at the memory before growing still, watching the highway. "Let them be."

"Yesterday was successful," Poppa T says, riding shotgun and resting his eyes. "Today was spiritually rich."

THE REAL

The Resurrection Tour had its problems. Big ones. At one church they visited, the local priest had to allay fears by telling his church to think of the HipHopEMass as services in a foreign language. They wouldn't be upset by mass in Spanish, would they?

In Charlotte, Lyn Holt, the youth ministries coordinator at St. Peter's Episcopal Church, one of the tour's host churches, refused to take the young people to the HipHopEMass, organizing instead a trip to the Discovery Museum next door for an exhibit on the Dead Sea Scrolls. While there was plenty of time to do both, she insisted it was "too full a day to take the kids to the hip-hop."

Waiting at the entrance to the exhibit beneath the King James version of Isaiah 40:3 — "Prepare ye the way of the Lord, make straight in the desert a highway for our God" — she complained, "We're assaulted from every side, us traditionalists. What about Beethoven and Mozart as part of our liturgy? Are they showing the kids the beauty of our great Episcopal heritage?"

Handing tickets out to her charges, she invoked the old metaphor of the three-legged stool of reason, scripture, and tradition upon which the faith ostensibly rests. "I'm afraid this hip-hop mass is kicking legs off the stool," she explained, her voice gracious yet anxious.

Just inside the entrance to the exhibit, a timeline contextualized the discovery and religious meaning of the Dead Sea Scrolls. Marked among the significant dates was the suicide of Socrates in 399 BCE, condemned for "undermining tradition," and c. 480 BCE–70 CE when "ritual purity was of the greatest importance" for Jews of the Second Temple era. Near the exit, the exhibition text noted how the Dead Sea Scrolls illustrate "different streams" of biblical texts until arriving at the "preferred" canon that is now known as the Hebrew Bible.

⌒☙⌒

As Kurtis says, faith is a process, not a dogma. Right-wing shock jock Bill Cunningham didn't get the memo. In Raleigh on the first full day of the tour, Poppa T was interviewed live on the air by the well-known radio personality. Almost immediately, Cunningham began playing offensive hard-core rap, the language raw and uncensored since the program was airing on satellite radio.

"I'm disappointed you'd play that to your listeners, Bill," Poppa T said, his usual high-octane enthusiasm flagging only for a moment. "If you were one of my kids in the South Bronx, you'd have a time out right now."

The shock jock persisted in equating the genre with the message, ignoring the priest's explanations. When he started mocking both hip-hop and the ministry, the priest decided to talk above him to his listeners. "Those people who don't like hearing Spanish or hip-hop at the altar don't realize that those stately old hymns America sings on Sunday were beer hall tunes Martin Luther brought into the church," he managed to get out before the interview ended abruptly.

⌒☙⌒

And then there were the musicians. He knew some of them thought of it as a gig instead of a ministry. So be it. But they would have to at least *act* like it was a ministry because, in fact, it was. He and Kurtis had been clear on that since the beginning. Some of the younger guys, however, wanted to blow off a little steam. They were working hard for very little money and didn't always feel like making nice with the church folk after a long day on the road, lugging equipment, playing long sets, and breaking down again.

"What started as a nice church program has grown into a national evangelistic crusade," was how Poppa T explained his position. "Certain standards of conduct and behavior aren't up for compromise. Our punctuality, sexual conduct, substance abuse, and how we act and don't act at concerts, these are becoming more formal procedures. When it comes to hip-hop, we have a reputation to counter and the last thing we can afford is to slip up because of someone's behavior. We have to show folks we're serious about what we stand for and preach about."

Julio and David Burnett, the Godfather, tried to mediate, but they weren't chaperones or the hip-cop cops, and the other musicians were not deacons. Unfortunately, going off book wasn't Poppa T's strong suit, as was clear when Kurtis diverged from the program at the first street mass and Bishop Roskam had to calm him down and remind him to let the spirit carry them all. Life on tour was even more foreign and chaotic. His attempts at churchlike authority and discipline as tour manager were irritating the tired musicians. The priest's tireless work ethic and organizational skills that were indispensable in making the whole Resurrection Tour happen began to feel oppressive on the road.

"Poppa T can go to the 'my-way-or-the-highway' place pretty quickly," D-Cross said with a grin and then would say no more.

On the last night of the tour, at an Episcopalian retreat center in the lush hills of Virginia beside an outdoor fire, the rappers, musicians, and priest hashed it out. Poppa T insisted everyone should speak, even though it was very late and they had been up since 4:00 a.m. Several of the musicians had wanted to drive back to New York immediately following the service, but after some exhausted complaints they stayed.

The Godfather listened to the priest's concerns and the musicians' beefs. When it was his turn to speak, he acknowledged that Poppa T's concerns were legitimate, then added, "All respect, Poppa T, but God's our booking agent on this one, not you."

"I can be an uptight guy at times," the priest acknowledged, "but let's do our job. The integrity of leadership — all our leadership — requires in this ministry an extra pound or two of care when it comes to certain subjects. I want everyone to know that none of us are indispensable. Not bishops, not priests, not musicians. This ministry stops for no one."

⤫

Money was tight. Always. The priest was good at stretching a dime, but still some, like Glory, had decided they could no longer afford to take on responsibility for the ministry without payment. Sometimes the musicians could not be paid on time, causing serious hardship. Others, like Jahneen, D-Cross, and Kurtis, got little more than expenses covered.

The ministry had its angels. The Sunday following his ordination, the Reverend Scot McComas, one of Poppa T's Harvard Divinity School classmates, designated the offering at his first service as a priest for the HipHopEMass. The contribution in August 2004 amounted to over $5,000 and allowed the summertime street ministry to resume at Trinity that fall as the HipHopEMass. Still, the more effective the ministry became, the more invitations it accepted and lives it touched, the more it needed to travel and grow and spend.

Back at Trinity, Poppa T was able to sustain the ministry the same way a family juggles the household budget, sometimes dipping into the grocery fund to keep the lights on or buy school supplies. The money was always accounted for, but, like any growing family with a meager income, Trinity's funds sometimes temporarily kept the HipHopEMass from going to bed hungry. When Paula found out that Trinity's budget occasionally carried the ministry over a shortfall, she was incensed.

It didn't matter that the money was always replaced. For her it was one more indication that the hip-hop ministry was increasingly insinuating itself into the life and budget of Trinity and becoming its priest's primary concern.

Poppa T saw it the same way Matthew 23:23 saw it: "Woe to you, scribes and Pharisees, hypocrites! For you tithe mint, dill, and cumin, and have neglected the weightier matters of the law: justice and mercy and faith. It is these you ought to have practiced without neglecting the others." As far as he and the Book of Matthew understood it, Trinity and the HipHopEMass had the same mission, the same life: to minister to the stranger, the sick, those in prison. Jesus said whatever you do to the least of these you do to me. If the choice was between money for polishing silver or outreach to those in the 'hood and prison who are strangers to God's word, well then, there really was no choice at all.

Now on the road, however, as the Resurrection Tour was coming to an end, it was running on financial fumes.

⁂

The priest was an easy target for much of the criticism. His progressive theology and belief in hip-hop as a prophetic African American appropriation of the Bible nettled many of the church ladies. His race and religion made him suspect to those rappers who wanted to "keep it real." Charismatic and larger-than-life, his intensity and passion for the ministry inspired but sometimes overwhelmed those who worked with him. And his sexuality remained an issue for critics in both the worlds of religion and hip-hop.

"In a lot of ways, race and sexuality are an issue," D-Cross offered in his easy, uncomplicated way. "They're talked about, and Poppa T is very aware of that. He said, 'Here I am, a big ol' white guy fronting a hip-hop mass.' Sometimes it can be an issue for hip-hop, given the history of how hip-hop came from city centers but white music executives controlled the purse strings. But those guys had no genuine concern for the culture and lives of the people who went along with it. I've sat with Poppa T. He's serious about reaching his young parishioners. He's concerned about their lives and culture."

Still, even among the most committed supporters and members of the HipHopEMass, Poppa T sometimes hit a wrong note. His unintentional misuse of hip-hop slang and juggernaut personality were easily indulged and often a source for good-natured and affectionate bemusement. His stubborn streak and Episcopal penchant for hierarchy were sometimes harder to take, especially when it came to the nature and expression of hip-hop itself. In particular, Poppa T's insistence on using a hip-hop Twenty-Third Psalm, despite objections to its authenticity by some of the HipHopEMass crew created some tension.

"We talked to him about the hip-hop version of the Twenty-Third Psalm and he says regardless of what we think he's still going to do it," says Paradox, one of the rappers at the very first HipHopEMass after it moved from the street into the church. "So that's how much he believes in what he's doing, because it's not just us. He has other people laugh at him, or laugh when they hear that version of Psalm 23. But you know, he believes in it so much that he says he's going to do it regardless."

"It's dated," agrees D-Cross but acknowledges that the priest has reasons beyond sheer stubbornness. "Poppa T explained that a young person who was ill wrote this adaptation so I didn't have a problem. Someone can look and say, this is corny. I probably would've wrote it different, but the language changes every other day. What might have been happening is not poppin' the next week."

Jahdiel and Monk of the Missionary Men and Rock were also at Trinity for the first HipHopEMass indoors. Like Paradox, they believe the priest's heart is in the right place but worry about his single-mindedness.

"In certain environments it does hurt the credibility of the whole movement," says Jahdiel, "because when you go on to real hard core...see, we're dealing with the children of the projects. You go into the real, real hard core where people are still gangbanging, people are still selling drugs and then they hear something like that...." He shrugs, as if there are no words. "It sounds like you're trying to mock them or imitate them. It's insulting them, basically. And we had people come up to us in Virginia and upstate New York and other places and say, 'It was nice, but that part was corny.' So that's another reason we brought it to him more than once."

"He's persistent," adds Rock with a meaningful smile.

⎯⎯⎯⎯⎯⎯

The social conservatives, church traditionalists, and hip-hop purists were not the only ones to misunderstand or mock what the HipHopEMass crew was up to. Well-meaning parishioners at predominantly white suburban churches they visited seemed to think of the ministry as a gimmick as well. In preparation for one service, enthusiastic middle-class white parishioners talked about sporting bling for the service the way they might discuss costumes for a Halloween party.

As the ministry grew, the fine line between being receptive and being condescending became a tightrope. In seeking to embrace and incorporate the rap ministry, were these well-meaning churches in danger of appropriating and demeaning what made it genuinely hip-hop and uniquely suited to speak?

Hip-hop had gone through the same tension when it grew beyond its local roots, becoming a major business. Some people say rap died when it moved from park jams and block parties to vinyl and the popular culture, its cultural significance growing but at the cost of co-option and exploitation. While purists may believe that hip-hop's resonance depends on its relevance beyond its 1970s origins and the borders of the South Bronx, they also see its global impact as a Faustian bargain struck by hip-hop's earliest pioneers ready and eager for props, cash,

and reps beyond the Bronxdale Projects or the Manhattan gal-
leries and nightclubs like the Roxy that embraced them. Money
made it hard to keep it real.

It was starting to look as if evangelizing was no different.
The HipHopEMass was now facing the same dilemma: how
to stay true to the roots of the street ministry, how to speak
the prophetic message to those who really only wanted a new
sound? Just as Tupac's spiritual and political diagnosis of the
"thug life" became diluted into the upper middle-class suburban white kid's "thug style," a turntable and good intentions
could allow churches across America to pose as urban projects
for the night while missing the point entirely.

Just as with hip-hop itself, the success of the HipHopEMass
put it in danger of losing its prophetic soul and its power to
change lives. After all, what was the point of filling pews if the
radical love of Jesus wasn't in the house?

Sincerity is not the same thing as authenticity, and for all of
Poppa T's sincerity, the man needed the authenticity of Kurtis,
D-Cross, D.O., Jahneen, Cool Clyde, the Missionary Men, the
Remnant, and the others to move the message and to fulfill
one of the ministry's original goals of "representing the home
of hip-hop — the South Bronx USA — to honor and celebrate
the roots of our culture — love, pride, and respect — through
DJing, MCing, art, spirit, and cultural style!"

All of these hip-hop disciples were initially impressed and
carried along by the priest's sincerity. Now they needed to
carry him and impress upon him what made them real and
not just an evangelical tool. They believed it was possible, that
the seeds were already there.

"There was one experience where I was outside with Monk
and this man walked by," Jahdiel explains, "and we was talking to him and he was drunk and he looked like he was taking
drugs. And then Poppa T came up and called him by his first
name and they were talking to each other. 'Hey, Tyrone!' He
had a relationship with all the young people in the neighborhood — and this is the ghetto. He knew everyone by name.

He knew their grandparents, parents, blood type, and they looked at him and they knew who he was, you know? That was impressive."

"It's kind of like our view of what a minister's supposed to be — and we do view ourselves as ministers also," adds Rock. "Yeah, he's a fifty-something-year-old white guy, but I mean, like, who cares what color he is? At the end of the day, he's reaching out to people, and that's what we're about."

"We saw that he was sincere about really trying to reach out to people and trying to do something to help his church," Paradox says. "Knowing his situation, you know, talking about the church dying, you know what I'm saying? Not really having membership, and especially that core group that gets in trouble at fifteen — what is it now, fifteen-to-thirty-year-old group? That's missing in most churches, and he addressed that, he acknowledged that it is a problem in the church, and he's trying to do something about it. You know? This is the reason a lot of churches do call us to come in. They don't know how to reach that age group in their community so they get us. We talk in their language, you could say."

❧

Despite the problems, the misunderstandings, the resistance from traditionalists, and the growing pains of the ministry and those who ran it, the Resurrection Tour built momentum. For some, mostly young people like Justin in Chapel Hill and Nicholas and Steffan in Durham, it was a revelation. For others, like Lyn Holt and Robert Patton, seventy-two, of Charlotte, it was a crying shame if not an outright abomination.

Mr. Patton, a formal African American gentleman, his gray hair and beard just a few shades lighter than his suit, sat in the very top row of the school bleachers in a Charlotte suburb with his "grands," Jerome, ten, and Lamar, eight, along with their friend Oryan, ten. As other children ran around in brand-new, oversized T-shirts reading "HipHopEMass Easter Resurrection Tour" on the front and "God's Got My Back!" on the back,

Jerome and Lamar, also dressed in suits and ties as if going to Sunday meeting, sat quietly with Oryan in the row in front of Mr. Patton.

He came because of his grandsons and because he always participated in his neighborhood and this was a neighborhood event. Besides, he had to admit he was a little curious to see what this hip-hop gospel was all about. It was his first time hearing about such a thing.

As the EMass band warmed up, though, he winced at the decibels. Although everyone around them was on their feet or on the floor of the gymnasium surrounding the rappers, Mr. Patton and the boys remained in their seats. Not more than fifteen minutes into the service, a hundred young people jumping up and down as the Remnant rapped "Unbelievable!" Mr. Patton had had enough. He guided the three boys down the bleachers, through the crowd and out the doors at the other end of the gym. Only Oryan looked back.

LOCKDOWN

"I'm just an ordinary middle-aged white gay hip-hop priest," he drawls. And then the laugh. Booming. Theatrical even. But Poppa T isn't joking. He climbs from the van outside the James River Juvenile Detention Facility in Maidens, Virginia, outside of Richmond, lugging his vestments as the rappers and musicians pull turntables and mikes from the second van.

This is the penultimate stop of the Resurrection Tour, but in many ways it is the reason the HipHopEMass crew has traveled so far, slept so little, and rapped so much. The expansive lawns and clean, low-rise architecture are deceiving. This is lockdown. Beyond the lawn, hidden by the freshly painted structures, is a ten-foot-high chain-link fence topped with razor wire surrounding an asphalt basketball court for the detainees. Visitors must pass through a metal detector and are buzzed in through two sets of metal doors. Inside the institutional block walls are numbered signs posted out of numerical order:

1. James River Behavior Program will be implemented throughout the day.

2. Sit at your desk and remain seated.

3. All 4 desk legs will remain on the floor.

5. All materials must be maintained at your desk.

6. Comply with staff directions at all times.

8. Keep your hands to yourself.

7. No name calling, cursing, or other use of inappropriate language or gestures.

4. No talking; raise your hand before speaking.

There are no unlocked doors anywhere, not in the classrooms, not in the cafeteria. As the EMass crew is shown to the gymnasium to set up, a guard must buzz them through each passageway and area of the complex. The threat of rain has pushed the service indoors into a small gym just big enough for a basketball court. At first glance, the gym looks as if it could belong in any small high school. Then the sound of a heavy metal door locking shut and the sight of three security booth windows where guards are watching suddenly make the space seem airless and cut off, as if underground.

Several poetic names — Alyssa, Maysheka, Ja'Quan among others — are written in capital letters on the Sports Restriction List taped to the security booth window. So far this is as close to the residents as the visitors have been allowed to come. D-Cross and Kurtis in particular seem humbled by their surroundings. These teenagers are the ones they have been waiting to meet.

Kurtis, having already set up his two silver decks, sits in the corner of the gym reading from the Book of Luke. "I'm just learning how to DJ," he confides. "Now I'm scratching for God!" He smiles. He's being polite, but clearly he does not want to talk. Not now. He's preparing himself to speak the Word of God. And this stop of the tour is very important to him. "We should have been doing this thirty years ago."

The staff at James River seems eager to welcome the rappers. Earlier, when greeting the crew, Pat Carrington, the senior supervisor, said, "We're blessed to have the HipHopEMass here." Another supervisor, BJ Johnson, chimed in, "We work hard at being among the chosen few."

They were not being facetious. They witnessed the ministry in 2004 when it visited Beaumont Juvenile Correctional Center just down the road. There, Kurtis, Poppa T, the Missionary

Men, Jahneen, and D-Cross ministered to Virginia's highest risk juvenile offenders, more than eighty boys and young men, including two on death row. It was the first time the HipHopEMass crew had gone to a prison. The priest did not know whether the teenage inmates "would laugh or stand in silence," but when he invited the whole room to come forward for anointing, no matter what they were thinking or feeling, a young prisoner, whose Brooklyn grandmother named him Amen, stepped forward.

As the Missionary Men rapped their version of Biggie's inspirational "Sky's the Limit," all the prisoners and another two dozen guards who had been posted around the gym were anointed that day. Paradox remembers many had tears in their eyes. Watching it all had been the president of the Southern Christian Leadership Conference, who later told the priest that the experience had been one of the most important days in his life. When the HipHopEMass received the Martin Luther King Jr. Leadership Award at the convention of the SCLC in January 2006, Rufus Whitfield, a juvenile counselor at James River, also known as 1DJX, found himself spinning at the turntable.

Yes, the priest thought of this as a homecoming. The anointing and laying on of hands at Beaumont in the first few months of the ministry had been significant, leading to an invitation at another death row prison in Virginia. Personally, the emotional and grateful response of the boy prisoners had helped Poppa T surmount any residual coyness he had about presenting himself as a hip-hop priest. The children and young people know a real thing when they see and experience it, he thought. If they understood and were touched by this ministry, he would not fail them.

Now back in Virginia, they had not been able to visit Beaumont again. However, the administration at James River invited the rappers to come to the sixty-bed facility for both boys and girls ranging in age from twelve to seventeen. As Julio and the musicians complete their sound check, Whitfield is explaining how the facility is a therapeutic environment. He is interrupted by the monotone voice and white noise of a nearby walkie talkie: "Please stop all movement."

~⊗~

The older boys file in first. Divided into groups dressed in either gray, blue, orange, or maroon sweats, corresponding to their resident pod and their age and grade, they enter single file, hands behind their backs, fingers intertwined. The girls enter next, also single file, right hand grasping the left forearm of the girl directly behind. There are only seven girls in two groups, distinguished by either gray sweatshirts or maroon polo shirts. Everyone is wearing immaculate white sneakers. Finally a small group of younger boys enters. Wearing dark blue pants and oversized bright orange sweatshirts, they look small and uncertain.

Agapé is spitting rhymes as the residents take their seats, but they don't speak or smile. No one knows why these kids are incarcerated — no one's allowed to ask — but behind the blank faces and studied indifference, the hip-hop disciples believe exists the soul of a generation. As Agapé finishes, D-Cross strides forward, his bulk and his presence so strong that when he shouts three times "Everybody throw up your hands!" all fifty-eight residents and the guards obey. The smaller boys in orange are embarrassed and after a few tentative waves in the air suddenly don't know what to do with their hands. Within a few beats, all the other hands are lowered as well. Only two girls in the front row keep waving their arms in the air until they notice they are alone and yank them down quickly, as if they touched fire.

D-Cross tries a new tack. "When I say, 'Amen,' you say, 'Word!' " At first there is silence. The expressionless residents, still seated in white plastic chairs, seem to be unsure as to what is expected of them or if they can really say anything at all. Then D-Cross starts shouting "Amen!" and pointing the mike at each of the separate groups as they say, "Word!" Soon he has them in an old school battle, each group trying to out "Word" the other, and when he's finished D-Cross feels as if "we won 'em over."

The residents start to loosen up, but it is perhaps Poppa T who has come most alive. He steps forward in his white vestments and the bright multicolored stole that Paula gave him. The residents are again completely still, watchful and uncertain about what's coming next. They sit in front of the priest, expressionless, giving away nothing.

"You see much hip-hop in me?" his amplified Southern-fried voice reverberates over the band's backbeat. The residents trade mocking glances or uncertain stares at the bald, flushed fifty-year-old priest who looks like he's wearing a dress. They have been told to be on their best behavior, but they shout out a loud, collective "No!"

"Well, I'm hip-hop today." They laugh again, but this time it's different, almost genuine. Poppa T is just warming up. "I don't rap. I don't dance, but I know love, so I know hip-hop!"

He knows they are looking to one another to see if it's okay to clap, to laugh, to pray. He even knows they may see him as a holy fool, a portly white guy in religious drag. But he also knows that for many of them this is different. They can trust the messengers. If not him, they can trust D-Cross. They can trust Kurtis and Kanye, Tupac and Jahneen. They can trust Agapé and D.O. and Nas and Mase. These are their people. These are their first prophets.

～≋～

"If you love the Lord, raise your hands," Kurtis says softly, standing behind his deck, but his amplified voice echoes in the gym. The residents are quiet, but he sees almost every hand raised. "C'mon," he says, much louder this time, working them up. "If you *really* love the Lord, let me hear some praise right now!"

To applause and some cheers he says, "Amen. Word!" The residents are openly looking at each other. They are being told to abandon their institutional reserve, break rule #4, and make some noise. Some remain expressionless or look skeptical, but others seem to brighten and a few even smile, daring to trust the moment.

"Spit it out while in lockdown, spit it out for God's love!" D-Cross shouts out, taking center court again. As he and D.O. start rapping "Jesus Walks," there is some spontaneous clapping, but it is reserved, polite, as if the detainees are obeying the rules of attendance.

When Poppa T starts to pray, they all hunch forward, some with elbows on their knees. Four or five of the boy prisoners, however, slump back in their chairs, hands on chins, cocky and skeptical. Then D-Cross steps forward again, one of the colorful EMass prayer cards with the controversial hip-hop Twenty-Third Psalm in his hand. The EMass band kicks in and the Living Instrument instructs the crowd to respond "That's what's up" after each line as he starts rapping and beatboxing:

> *The Lord is all that,*
> *I need for nothing.*
> *He allows me to chill.*
> *He keeps me from being heated*
> *And allows me to breathe easy.*
> *He guides my life*
> *So that I can represent*
> *And give shouts out in his Name.*
> *And even though I walk through*
> *the 'Hood of death,*
> *I don't back down*
> *For you have my back.*
> *The fact that he has me covered allows me to chill.*
> *He provides me with back-up*
> *In front of my player-haters*
> *And I know that I am a baller*

And life will be phat.
I fall back in the Lord's crib
For the rest of my life.

Again, the crowd responds to D-Cross, his talent and his spirit. Even Kurtis, who has seen them all, calls him "incredible." Even though D-Cross still felt this hip-hop Twenty-Third Psalm was "dated," the Living Instrument invested it with respect. He found the spirit in it and the young inmates — "the residents," as the James River staff calls them — seem to find it too. By the time Kurtis steps from behind his two decks to preach, the gym is quiet and focused. They want to hear what the King of Rap has to say. What he says first is a prayer.

"Lord, make me decrease so you can increase," he almost whispers, the microphone so close his breathing itself is part of the prayer. "Help me bring a message to my brothers and sisters here today that you are real and will forgive and are worthy of praise. Amen."

Followed by a whispered "Word."

There is a long silence. Prisoners, residents, inmates, children — whoever these boys and girls are, whatever they are called, they are waiting, perhaps even hoping, to hear something that is real, that can tell them who they are.

" 'For you, O Lord, are good and forgiving, abounding in steadfast love to all who call on you.' " Kurtis closes the Bible. Everyone is watching him. He looks into the faces and sees them. Whatever concern he may have had before about what to say or how to say it seems to vanish. He sees them.

He begins with the Moses story, the remixed street version, rapidly getting to the point that "the Hebrews hollered at God. You gotta holler at your boy. We're out in the wilderness like the Hebrews in Exodus, and like them we have to change our lives, let God transform us."

It's a sermon, but no one is close to falling asleep. He tells them about the roots of hip-hop, about the landlords setting

fire to people's homes for insurance money and how the children tried to make something beautiful on the other side of
the burned-out street, how it wasn't about the thug life but
about creating a better life, how the first graffiti artists would
spray paint "Up with Hope! Down with Dope!" right where
the drug dealers and junkies could see it. The man who used
to perform in front of 150,000 people and on television is giving everything he's got to these fifty-eight kids in lockdown
off a country road. They, and their guards, are rapt. He stops
pacing, stills his gesturing hands, and turns to the assembly.

"Sooner or later you gonna go home," he says finally, and
even though nobody moves the words seem to galvanize the
boy and girl prisoners. "I guarantee it. I pray you don't come
back here. But what's gonna ensure you don't end up back here
when you get out? What's gonna keep you free?" Kurtis again
looks into their faces and then states simply, urgently, into the
microphone, fist clenched, "Holler. At. Your. Boy."

He starts moving again, crossing the basketball court like a
preacher hauling brimstone. "There's a Greek word in philoso-
phy," he says. "*Telos.* It means purpose. What is your purpose,
your end? What is the purpose of your life? The *telos* of an
acorn is to become an oak tree. The *telos* of a caterpillar is to
become a butterfly. What is your *telos?* Is it money, women,
drugs, success? I've had all that stuff. None of it made me
happy."

Two boys in the gray pod exchange quick, incredulous looks,
as if that's exactly what would make them happy.

"I was rap's first millionaire, the first rapper signed to a
major label." He raises an arm, lifts his chin, puffing up as
if accepting applause. Just as rapidly, he drops them. "I had
everything. I just wanted more. Drugs? I just wanted more.
Women? Sex? I just wanted more. I still wasn't happy. The
first time I got happy was when I got God in my life. I found
my *telos.* Find your *telos.* Ask God what it is. Holler at your
boy! He will give you another chance. It ain't too late. It ain't
too late for you, it ain't too late for me, you know? God is a

God of the second, third and fourth chance. Go for it. Holler at your boy."

Kurtis drops the microphone, and as Jahneen's soulful vocal and the Godfather's blues riff lead the EMass band into "Sweet Jesus," Poppa T steps forward.

"Anyone here in need of prayer?" he asks. Surprisingly, it is the older teenage boys of the blue pod who raise their hands, almost without exception. Only one or two others in each of the other groups do so.

Then, in a HipHopEMass tradition begun back at Trinity, the priest invites them all to step forward for anointing and laying on of hands. While the ritual as provided for in the Book of Common Prayer is usually reserved for adults who presumably "understand" the significance of anointing, Poppa T believed the children and young people not only could understand but honestly yearned deeply for the healing, hope, and blessing of the Holy Spirit. He was criticized for it, but in the South Bronx and on the road they came forward, little children and gang bangers, to communicate in this way with God.

Now Kurtis, Poppa T, D-Cross, Jahneen, Agapé, D.O., and Beaumont's chaplain stand in a line facing the crowd. Again, a few older boys lead the way. The two teenagers who kept checking in with one another and the hand-waving girls slouch further down into their chairs, but almost everyone else in each pod follows the older boys and lines up in front of the hip-hop disciples.

The gym is subdued but no longer in institutional torpor. Rather, the basketball court has become a church for these few moments, the young residents calmed in thought, in something interior not mediated by rules, signs on the wall, or guards and supervisors. As the soft blues chords of "Sweet Jesus" wash over them, they bow heads, accept blessings and the touch of the disciples' hands. Several of the young prisoners tower over the HipHopEMass crew and have to stoop.

The rappers and clergy, speaking in whispers as if not wanting to disturb the fragile trust that's been created, ask the teenagers their names and what they want to pray for. One wants to pray for a successful court date, one for her baby back home. Another prays for a lost mother. Many ask forgiveness for crimes and sins. All want prayers for family.

Jahneen tells the girls they are beautiful, to not give up on themselves. "If God could help me," she says, "he will work miracles for you." She tells them she was a real hard case and that even though it might not sound logical to be told to keep your head up while in lockdown, one day they'd be out and they need to keep a sense of how special they are.

Before returning to their seats, Jahneen gives everyone hugs that they accept shyly, gratefully. About five teenagers from the gray pod surround Kurtis and instead of folding their hands in prayer, they hold out their fists and pound knuckles. The King of Rap's eyes are shut tight, his face gleaming with sweat and spirit.

As the last few boys lined up in front of Kurtis and D-Cross return to their seats, Poppa T leads all fifty-eight residents in the Confession from the hip-hop prayer card:

Merciful God
We confess we have sinned against you and our neighbor.
We have not done right by you.
We have not done right by other people.
We are sorry.
We want to change . . .

When they are finished, the priest raises his arms to embrace them all. "Whatever you've thought, whatever you've done, God forgives you. He loves you. He doesn't make mistakes. When he created you he didn't make a mistake. You are forgiven. It's a done deal."

As the EMass band softly plays, the hip-hop disciples go into the crowd, giving the guys a pound, bumping shoulders, and shaking hands. Agapé and Jahneen give motherly hugs that embarrass some of the boys, but most accept them eagerly.

Some of them are fighting back emotion. With others it's hard to tell. They all seem deep in thought.

Long after Poppa T has called everyone back to the Eucharist table, Kurtis stands in back with one boy in blue, still praying. D-Cross keeps moving through the gym, among the blue and the gray and the maroon and the orange, until he has taken the hand of everyone present. He forgets no one. He touches them all.

Before the HipHopEMass crew left James River that day, everyone was dancing. It was the blues who started rocking in their seats, then on their feet — the guards gave them permission — after Rufus Whitfield waved his hand in the air and started in with some old school moves. By the time Kurtis finally rapped his version of Snoop Doggs "Beautiful" — "Oh, Lord, you're beautiful" — followed by his own classic hits, bodies were swaying, hands were clapping, and everyone, including the holdouts from the orange pod, was having a good time.

After the service, in a classroom with furniture bolted to the floor, a seventeen-year-old girl from the maroon pod, one of only two girls who didn't go forward for anointing said, "This felt real."

"When you hear Kurtis Blow, it's from the heart," said a teenage boy, a dark tuft sprouting on his chin.

"It really moved me," offered another boy with dark blond hair. "It gave me a feeling I only get when. . . . " He touches his chest and doesn't finish the sentence, open and vulnerable in a way that can't be safe here.

The tall seventeen-year-old who had to stoop for anointing agreed. "People gonna stereotype us and hip-hop," he said. "Something like the HipHopEMass makes a difference here."

"It's got to," another boy prisoner added. "If we don't change. . . . " He gazes over his shoulder, as if looking for the horizon but all there is behind him is a locked metal door. When he turns back, he makes eye contact. "I been here a few."

"At James River, that's something that stirs me to this day," D-Cross said almost one year later in his classroom at P.S. 751 in the East Village. "I ran into one of the young men last summer, back in the Bronx, after he got out of detention in Virginia. He said thank you. That one afternoon, he said, helped him deal and cope with his time there. I was like, wow. That experience was the highlight of all of the HipHopEMasses for me, more than all the other tours and services."

THE BREAKS

To: Lillas Bogle, Senior Warden
Keith Warren, Junior Warden

From: Paula A. Roberts

Date: June 13, 2006

I need to express my thoughts and outrage at the state of Trinity Church of Morrisania. I am calling for:

1. An immediate end to Hip Hop being associated with Trinity Episcopal Church of Morrisania, including: (A) using or linking the church's name with Hip Hop/Hip Hop e mass (B) completely refraining from using Trinity church for photographing Hip Hop as a ministry or for any other promotional or media exposure (C) that there be an immediate refrain from connecting Trinity Church of Morrisania from Hip Hop in any way.

2. Remove the name of Trinity Church of Morrisania, Bronx, from any current and future publications, such as articles, books, promotions, advertisement, or anything associated with Hip Hop.

3. Now that Father Holder has established Hip Hop as his ministry, I propose that he now completely sever his ties from Trinity and continue to establish his ministry elsewhere.

4. That all restricted funds cease being used for any other purpose other than what they have been allocated for and that all monies borrowed from the restricted fund account be returned immediately.

It is my belief that Rev. Timothy Holder has and continues to use and exploit the outstanding name and reputation that Trinity Church in the Bronx has had for 138 years. He has done this for his own personal advancement and grandiosity. Trinity is now known as the "Hip Hop Church" in and around the city and country. Our rector is now referred to as "Papa Tim," "the rapper," as quoted by 1010 WINS news. I cannot believe that as wardens and the members of the vestry you are proud of this identity. I am not. I am outraged and profoundly saddened at how our church has been destroyed by the current rector and how the wardens and vestry have allowed this to continue, being oblivious to what is really taking place in front of your eyes. It is clear that "Papa Tim" has established a name for himself at our expense and should now separate his ministry from that of Trinity of Morrisania. Are we going to continue to support him financially so that he may continue to build his own empire at Trinity's expense? He is spending enormous amounts of time that should be allotted to building ministry at Trinity while promoting himself.

One must ask: how or what has Trinity gained or accomplished over the past three years? Financially, we are worse off than we have ever been, to the point of receiving cut-off notices from utility companies. This cannot all be blamed on the unfortunate deaths that have occurred within the parish, which have been numerous. With the number of baptisms that have taken place over the past three years, why are the pews still empty? Why do we still not have a viable Sunday School program? While it may be impressive to quote large numbers, we have nothing to show for it. You are aware that some parishioners have withdrawn their financial support as a means of silent protest. How can you account for less than forty parishioners attending service when Bishop Taylor conducted his visitation of the parish, with the understanding that he was coming to perform the sacrament of confirmation, only to find out that there were no conferments? It is well known that whenever Bishop Taylor or any bishop visits Trinity that the pews are filled to capacity with great excitement generated, including a royal banquet. This was not the case this year.

With much thought and prayer, I have agonized about my place at Trinity and what I am not getting spiritually. I realize that I have come to the place where I need to make some very difficult and painful decisions about where I will get my spiritual fulfillment, as Trinity is not meeting my needs under the present leadership. While I am speaking for myself, I know that I am also expressing the sentiments for those who suffer in silence, and are feeling powerless.

Cc: The Rt. Rev. Mark S. Sisk
    The Rt. Rev. E. Don Taylor
    The Rev. Canon John Osgood
    The Rev. Timothy Holder
    Members of the Vestry
    Trinity Congregation

THE FUTURE PAST

Paula had given a lot of thought to what she needed to say. "As a minority woman in white culture," she said, "I learned to speak up. All my life I've had to fight."

The meetings, the explanations, Glory's testimony, the growing national reach of the ministry, none of it persuaded her that hip-hop was a gift from God to her church. If her father's successor could not see how this rap ministry was violating the Episcopal spirit of high church worship, he could not avoid seeing that it was tearing Trinity apart.

The congregation, by which she meant those who supported her, had had enough. She had had enough. She signed her name and addressed her letter to Mr. Warren and Lillas Bogle. She also sent copies to her parents' dear friend and fellow Jamaican Don Taylor, the bishop of New York, as well as Bishop Sisk, Poppa T, and the entire congregation. She pointedly left Bishop Roskam off the list. As far as Paula was concerned, there was no point cc:ing the woman known as the hip-hop bishop and who Poppa T in mock solemnity declared "first in line in the hip-hop apostolic succession."

This was not the first time Trinity experienced upheaval because of churchmanship, ritual, and foreign faces in the pews. It wasn't even the first time an impassioned letter was dispatched from the parish to the bishop of New York about a controversial priest. From 1880 until 1923, Trinity's congregation was displaced from their recently completed church building at the corner of 166th and Trinity Avenue. On the surface, the young church was simply a victim of the Panic of 1873 that sent the entire country into a depression. Unable to refinance its mortgage, Trinity suffered foreclosure barely six years after its completion. Below the economic tide, however, were deeper, stronger currents. Some believed conflicting theologies and styles of worship were behind one faction of parishioners refinancing the original building out from under Trinity's rector, Reverend Albert Hull, and his loyal congregation.

Those who took over the neo-gothic structure renamed it Holy Faith Church. Considered "low church" by the Reverend Hull and his flock, they were evangelical in both spiritual outlook and practical outreach. The displaced churchgoers kept the name of Trinity Church, ultimately making a home in a smaller, wooden building on 164th Street only a few blocks away, where they preserved the staunchly high church style and traditions of the Anglican Communion. The congregational split resulted in the extraordinary creation of two separate and distinct Episcopal parishes only a few blocks apart.

While there is no formal record authorizing the split by officers of the diocese, it appears the neglect of such a necessary step did not keep the two factions from taking their God and going their respective ways. While both claimed membership in the Anglican Communion and fealty to the will of God, the two churches stood by their distinct characters as if standing by the one true cross.

For decades, Trinity Church existed in exile from its original home under Reverend Hull's pastoral care. In a letter written by the rector shortly after being forced to leave the church he had helped build, he expressed "great disappointment that all my work has come to this." Rallying like a good churchman, however, he went on to write that he would not be bitter, vowing instead to put his energy toward serving his congregation and taking Trinity Church elsewhere. And elsewhere is where they remained for forty-two years.

In 1923 the Trinity and Holy Faith congregations finally reunified. However, Reverend Hull never saw the gleaming wooden vaults and stained glass inside Trinity's original house of worship again. He had died the year before, after serving the staid, traditional congregation for fifty-two years. Today, a memorial window next to Trinity's sacristy door honors his long ministry and his defense of the high church ways.

Reverend Edward T. Theopold was never vindicated with a memorial window. His eighteen years of service as Trinity's fourth rector were marked by cultural friction, congregational factionalism, and open dissent. When he arrived at Trinity in 1932, the pews were filled with white descendants of the founding congregation. By the time World War II began, however, African American and Caribbean churchgoers had arrived in the South Bronx and at Trinity Church of Morrisania.

With its cornerstone set in the post–Civil War era, when Morrisania was still a village surrounded by farmland and the summer estates of New York's gentry, Trinity did not immediately welcome the new arrivals. Their way of doing things was considered too foreign and indefinably un-Episcopalian if not vaguely un-Christian. The church's old ways were inscribed on the congregation like commandments on stone tablets, and in the absence of a burning bush to introduce change, Trinity treated them as immutable laws. Any deviation simply aggravated the longtime parishioners' anxiety over change and focused the new parishioners' desire to assume their rightful spiritual and social leadership within the community and church.

By all accounts Father Theopold did not hesitate in trying to integrate the newcomers. He worked hard to accommodate the various allegiances and needs of the different cultural factions, mediating arguments over everything from rules for using church facilities to ethnic intrusions onto the church banquet menu. It became clear to everyone except perhaps the priest himself that the two factions, having staked their positions, would not be reconciled.

The remnant of the predominantly white congregation wanted the priest gone; the new Caribbean congregation embraced him as he had embraced them and wanted him to stay. Things became so contentious that finally, in 1946, the vestry addressed a letter to the then-bishop of New York, William Thomas Manning:

> During the past month there has been a subtle campaign by a few misled and disloyal members of Trinity to destroy the harmony and to retard the progress of the work being so effectively carried on by our rector, Rev. Edward Theopold.
>
> In fact, this group has gone so far as to be making strenuous efforts to secure signatures for the removal of Rev. Theopold as rector.
>
> We, the vestry, have recently renewed our pledge of loyalty to our rector and we are here asking the congregation to do likewise.
>
> We, the vestry, are fully satisfied in the democratic way the finances and other affairs of the parish have been administered during the past critical days of the changeover from a white to a colored congregation, and in grateful recognition of the efforts and services rendered by Rev. Theopold in making the beautiful church ours, we pledge him our wishes that he may remain as our rector as long as God Wishes.

Signed: Rufus Gibson   Neilson Tomlinson
         Wilfred Nelson   Jamel Cumberbatch &
         Frank O. Davis   E. Seon

Bishop Manning responded by asking Father Theopold to split his energies between Trinity and Emmanuel Chapel over

on Cortland Avenue. Finally, in 1950 the overtaxed rector resigned, the last white priest to serve the final descendants of
Trinity's founding members.

Morrisania was a Puerto Rican, black, and Caribbean community now, overflowing with the flavors, energy, and sounds
of a cultural Diaspora that would earn the Bronx an affectionate sobriquet as the "Borough of Salsa y Meringue." Jazz,
calypso, mambo, R&B, reggae, soul, be-bop, and other African-
and Latin-style sounds filled the streets long before the arrival
of scratch and rap. Through open windows on hot summer
nights, the sounds of Benny Goodman, Doris Day, and Frank
Sinatra that were popular with the remaining Irish, Italian and
Jewish residents gave way to Tito Puente, Elmo Hope, and
Thelonius Monk, who at some point all lived and played in
the South Bronx.

When Father Roberts arrived in 1950 from Jamaica, formal-
izing Trinity's transition to a black church, it finally settled the
question of who belonged and who didn't. The man at the altar
looked like the people in the street. The people who lived and
worked in the neighborhood now filled the pews. The young
priest wasted no time electing a new, all black vestry and began
putting behind the controversies and tension that had wracked
Trinity for almost a generation. But the past rarely stays where
it belongs, and Father Roberts's widow and daughter would find
themselves reliving Trinity's painful transition a half century
later, only this time they would be the ones resisting the new
faces, strange accents, and unfamiliar ways.

⸎

God wants us to hear him. That's the message of prophets and
seers alike. Glory heard him in his room rapping new rhymes.
Jahneen heard him on what she thought was her deathbed.
Kurtis heard him above the sirens and the incessant gangsta
beats. He speaks to us in ways we can understand. And we
come to him in the only way we know how. It is our way alone.

This is what all faithful sons and daughters ultimately understand. They have to find him on their own and hear him for themselves.

Millions hear him through the baroque hymns, reverent prayers, and formal Episcopal rituals like those Trinity has cherished for generations, through foreclosure and exile, riot and flames. But he has also started speaking through the MCs and DJs of hip-hop. Of this the rappers and the priest have no doubt.

They know that people can inherit religion, its majesty and traditions, but faith is singular and at times lonely. Too often the trappings of religion are mistaken or substituted for faith. Jesus told his followers and critics as much. It is the pitfall of every spiritual generation that many who speak and act in his name are often strangers to his love. They recite his word but do not heed his lessons.

Would the faithful deny their gifts to those who want to pray? Would they close the house of God to anyone looking for him because of the way they dress or speak or because, most ironic of all, they really truly need him and want to live differently?

Poppa T knew too well how there are always church people who say certain others have no place among them. As the first openly gay Episcopal priest ordained in Alabama, he knew a lot about those who try to control God and decide who does and doesn't belong in his church. In fact, the bishop who accepted him into the priesthood had previously denied ordination to other gay men. Now that same bishop called Poppa T his "point of redemption."

This was just another example of God's love getting bigger and bigger everyday, he believed, just as he believed the HipHopEMass expands that love. Everybody's welcome. Everybody. If anyone has a problem with God's love for everybody, then they've got a problem with God.

He didn't know how many times he used that line at the altar or in an interview, but for him it was as simple as that.

"I can think of nothing more troubling than going from a beautiful Catholic mass that many Episcopalians love, to a hip-hop mass," Poppa T acknowledged, trying to see Paula's side after reading her letter. "There are honest problems with it."

But it was a problem Christianity had already faced countless times and always overcome, he thought. Just as the Bible has been translated into the languages and dialects of the world from the original Aramaic and Greek, and Latin liturgies have given way to conversational speech, his church will find its future only by making itself understood to those who will make the future. He had faith it would. He again thought of Bishop Roskam and the words she wrote that first summer, "If Jesus were to come today, he would be a rapper."

How we live our faith says more about us than about God, the unorthodox say. In the priest's experience, they said it mostly at Harvard, but it was equally true in the PJs. Religious traditionalists have found meaningful expression of faith in their traditions, but for those who cannot relate or for whom those rites don't resonate, there is a need for rites that do. From the very first street service, the HipHopEMass has asked: do the faithful love their traditions more than they love their neighbor?

It's a fair question. In fact, he believed it was inevitable. The church has often had to choose between change and tradition. Ultimately, it is a spiritual decision, a journey of discernment that requires the faithful to look again at the imperatives of what they believe and the nature of God's will. The single-mindedness of youth and faith are not so different. Put into service of one another, together they have opened history to those who history would destroy or deny.

Not all the dreams of youth or beliefs of the faithful, however, are about love and justice. Still, when their hopes are bigger than their fears, when they are guided by their highest ideals, spiritual and cultural generations renew and inspire a deeper sense of what it means to be alive. When the talents of these new generations serve the needs of the world, justice and love do win.

"These kids, this Hip-Hop Nation, this mighty, strong, powerful nation is the future of the world," Kurtis had said at a rest stop on the Resurrection Tour. "It's the future of the church. It's our future ministers, our future elders and trustees as much as our future doctors, lawyers, presidents."

There are those who say it is not worth fighting the hip-hop church movement. It is a fad, they say, as fickle as hip-hop slang, and will soon be obsolete or disappear. Kurtis smiles but says nothing. The critics and clerics who denounced the growing hip-hop ministries for religious reasons or claimed rappers like him and Hammer, DMX and Reverend Run started rhyming about Jesus in order to revive dead careers, don't bother him. He tries not to think about the haters, saying simply, "We will soon learn if the Holy Spirit is with this ministry, if God wants this thing to happen."

Sitting at a back table at Sylvia's Soul Food in Harlem, not far from where he first found God and hip-hop, he quotes Acts 5:38–39 in the King of Rap version: " 'Keep away from these men because if what they do is about them, it's never going to work. But if what they do is about God, then you can never overthrow it. You just find yourself fighting against God.' "

As the waitress ferries glasses of sweet iced tea and hot plates of fresh corn bread to the end of the counter, he seems at peace. He is a licensed nondenominational reverend now, and when his cell phone rings, he answers, "The Minister Kurtis Blow Walker." He isn't worried about the nature of hip-hop. He came from its heart. He knows it is a gift from God.

Poppa T did not see Paula's letter for a few weeks. A few days before it was sent his mother died. Driving the old silver Taurus down to Elizabethton, Tennessee, staring at the interstate for hours, he was tired. Very tired. All the rancor over worship, all the controversy over hip-hop, all the effort to control the uncontrollable suddenly weighed on him like endless miles. As he drew closer to his boyhood home, the Taurus struggling to climb higher into the dusk of northeast Tennessee, the mountains turned the color of deep ocean water and he felt like he was floating.

He floated like that for several days, and on the morning of his mother's funeral, he stood at the pulpit of First Free Will Baptist Church and read her favorite Bible passage from the Book of John: "The wind blows where it chooses, and you hear the sound of it, but you do not hear where it comes from or where it goes. So it is with everyone who is born of the Spirit."

Despite his grief there was something freeing in the words. He did not know where the wind was going or where it would carry him, but for the first time it did not seem to matter. Let it blow. Let it take him where the Spirit chose even if that meant away from the South Bronx. He knew now it did not matter as long as God carried him. He felt a sense of release, comforting like the cleansing wind or a lesson from mother to son.

That afternoon, in a cemetery on a Tennessee mountainside, he cried. Beside the casket stood members of his family and the rural folk his mother had served as a nurse for fifty years. Among several arrangements blessing the grave was a bounty of flowers in all colors, the inscription reading, "Your HipHopEMass Family."

⤜≥⤏

"Oh, I've been criticized," Paula grins, eyes rolling, her tone implying volumes. "People have said that I forced him out, that I'm too outspoken, that I'm not allowing change to happen. I'm not going to be defensive about it — I didn't force Tim out. People say I'm very powerful and I am, but I'm not that powerful."

Behind the businesslike rigor of Paula's tone there is something melancholy and baffled. All she had wanted to do was defend the church she had always known and loved and to preserve it for those her father and Trinity's faithful had marched for and believed would rise from all they had suffered and sacrificed.

The Bronx had once been the breeding ground of influential antiracist activists, and the Morrisania branch of the NAACP had been its epicenter. But where was that generation of local doctors, lawyers, and clergy the old members of Trinity had tried to march and pray into existence? Where were those pretty girls in ball gowns and handsome well-spoken gentleman of the South Bronx in whom the future had held such promise? Instead, the generation that was forged in the burning of the South Bronx was not the one they had tried to raise and believed was coming. The thugs and the rappers came instead.

While she accepted that generational shift was inevitable, she could not accept that the time had come. Not yet. Please, God, not yet. She and the congregation would need more time. It was happening too fast and not in the right way, not by her way of seeing. The church was simply becoming increasingly unstable and its resources diminished. The children Father Timothy kept talking about failed to materialize in significant or consistent numbers. The nights of rap music failed to translate into Sunday morning religious instruction. And so she had tried to stop it.

When Forest Houses were built in the early 1950s, it literally shook the foundations of Trinity. Mrs. Roberts remembers the dynamite blasts during construction rattling the walls so many times it still makes her shake her head with a tight smile. Each of those blasts helped to sink the projects' foundations deeper into the South Bronx and loosen some of Trinity's gold leaf and plaster. The church was again being shaken to its core, this time by the explosion of hip-hop, and again it was a Roberts who stepped forward to save it.

The wheels were set in motion, and behind the scenes Poppa T had begun looking for another home for himself and the ministry. After several months of searching for a suit-able parish, in December 2006 Bishop Roskam encouraged the priest to "get on with it."

Even though the majority of the vestry had remained sup-portive of the rap ministry, two years marked by controversy and conflict were taking their toll on everyone. The priest knew that among the parishioners even the allies of the HipHopEMass had no real passion for rap. It was the chil-dren they cared about, and perhaps they were beginning to think that there were other ways to serve them through the afterschool and Sunday morning breakfast programs that were not necessarily about hip-hop. He couldn't blame them for wanting to put the turmoil to rest. Right before Christmas, he announced he was leaving Trinity come February.

"I didn't want to get fired, and there was a very real pos-sibility that could happen," Poppa T explained, referring to a potential vote of no-confidence by the vestry that is generally how rectors are dismissed in the Episcopal Church.

He accepted a post at the Historic Church of the Ascension just off the boardwalk in Atlantic City. It was also an aging commuter congregation, mostly white, elderly members in a poor African American 'hood, but the parishioners welcomed the possibility of new members from the surrounding streets and, more importantly, the promise of a hip-hop church.

Those who supported the priest and the hip-hop congrega-tion and did not want to see them go thought Paula was the villain. But there were no villains, Mr. Warren said, just as there were no saints. The priest and the daughter of a priest were just flawed human beings and, as with Trinity's faithful in previous generations, it had become too hard to disentangle their gen-uine religious differences from competing personal interests and cultural identities.

Still, for Paula the criticism was painful. At first she denied it, saying she never took any of the things people said person-ally, but one Sunday after church while heading to the hospital to squeeze in a few more hours of work, she had to admit that sometimes, not always, but sometimes it hurt. Of course, she added, "It depended on who it was coming from" and the vulnerable moment passed almost immediately as she steered her gleaming black Lexus SUV across the bridge into Manhattan. She was a strong woman. She only did what she felt needed to be done. She only said what she felt needed to be said. The rest . . . well, it is what it is.

She had stopped worshipping at Trinity shortly after a parishioner accused her of being a hypocrite in front of several other church members. Always gracious and gentle, Mrs. Roberts had rushed to her daughter's defense, but long before Poppa T resigned as rector, Paula had stopped attending the 11:00 a.m. Sunday service.

She claimed she wasn't getting what she needed spiritually at Trinity anymore. The message she needed to hear no longer resonated from inside those walls. And maybe, she conceded, a part of it was that she was getting the cold shoulder. Her coterie of supporters still looked to her for leadership, but other longtime members were sorry to see Poppa T go and made no bones about thinking it was Paula's fault. And so she left.

All the changes were sad. At least they made her sad. But then she scoffed at herself. After all, everyone always wants to recapture what they once had or felt or experienced, and the truth of it is that they're never going to. Things move on.

"It's almost like a death," she said pensively, as if just coming to the realization. "As people in the church are dying and getting older and fading away, you don't have what you once had. Going to church now, it's not the same as what we once had.

"I guess it was that excitement," she continued. Suddenly her eyes lit up and her voice became bright. "Yes, the excitement of going to church and of worshipping and feeling that good, great feeling. I don't really feel like I have it anymore. I think that's what makes me feel a bit sad."

She insists that her faith never wavered, but that great, good feeling proved elusive. She resigned from several committees within the diocese but not the Reparations Committee, which was studying the Episcopal Church's ownership of slaves and its involvement in the slave trade. It is the only remaining religious service position left as she tries to feel that excitement again in different pews among strange congregations. She's pulled way back. She's looking forward to traveling and more jazz concerts with the free time. It is what it is.

THE PROMISE

After the Resurrection Tour, Jahneen only served at Trinity's altar once more. That summer she joined the old crew for the second anniversary of what she, D-Cross, Kurtis, Cool Clyde, and the others had come to think of as the first HipHopEMass, when the storm chased them from the street into the church that would too briefly be their home. That would be the last HipHopEMass event at Trinity Church of Morrisania.

The following September, she resigned from the board, feeling exhausted by the incessant demands of the work, the controversies, and the personalities involved. At one point she was acting as treasurer, designing services with Poppa T, singing, and acting as MC for liturgies in addition to her work as musical director at St. Mark's in-the-Bowery.

"Like at the start of a love affair, you might know someone's faults but you want to be with them anyway," she says in the cramped office she shares with D-Cross at P.S. 751 in the East Village, where they both teach music. "I would be less than honest if I didn't say that had things been different I might have found the time."

A bell rings and the sound of students — the kind of teenagers social service agencies and the educational system call "at-risk" and most everyone else calls thugs — can be heard swarming through the building's warren of hallways and stairwells. For a moment she seems to be listening to her thoughts and not the classroom filling with loud laughter and trash talk just outside. "I realized I needed rest," she continues, "although some of those services were highlights of my life, like that day at the prison for youth offenders. Of course, there's always more money, but in terms of fulfilling God's purpose in life, it doesn't get any better than that."

At St. Mark's she still occasionally creates and leads hip-hop services, but rather than celebrating the full HipHopEMass, D-Cross comes into Manhattan and together they rap and sing and spread the word. There are no TV cameras, no radio interviews or newspaper reporters. To her own surprise, she realizes she never really liked that part of the ministry, just like she never liked when the priest would introduce her at HipHopEMass events as Queen Jahneen. She asked him to stop. It was embarrassing. It felt too much like the old days when she would have loved to be queen of something — anything. Now she was just Jahneen again. That's all she really wanted to be.

Still, the musicians all agreed that the rap service she first put together at St. Mark's back in 2001, and the connections she made for Poppa T were essential to the birth and growth of the HipHopEMass. Whenever D-Cross, Glory, Julio, Dave Burnett, or any of them spoke about Jahneen, their voices and expressions grew soft and they stammered like schoolboys. She did it first, and she was a queen in their eyes.

"She is the queen of hip-hop in the Episcopal Church," Poppa T whispered affectionately after she asked him to stop. "Just don't let her hear that."

She scoffs when she does hear it, but she cannot hide that smile. Then she shakes her head, casts those big brown eyes down while brushing imaginary lint from her stylish jeans and says confidentially, "A lot about religion makes us go outside ourselves — not to God — for approval and for control." Then she stops speaking, perhaps struck by the similarities between the music and religion industries. Or perhaps she does not want to criticize.

Instead, she says, "In my heart I believe God wants us to enjoy work, sex, living well. He wants us to uplift our lives and our race — the whole human race — and allows us to rest carefully when our time is up.... He did that for me. I felt like shit when I got here, but the HipHopEMass made me feel useful."

She doesn't miss the HipHopEMass — she's too busy with teaching, St. Mark's, and serving on the Episcopal Church's Standing Commission on Liturgy and Music — but sometimes she does miss the anointing of the children and the feeling of family among the other musicians and rappers. She loved everybody in that ministry, and she believes together they made good music and did good works. It couldn't have been that good, she believes — it just couldn't have been — without the love.

⌘

"I don't see myself as a preacher," D-Cross protests. "Despite what's been put out there a lot of times, I don't even see myself as a religious person. You can be a religiously bad person. A lot of people get caught up in liturgy and dogma and miss the words and the message. When I sit down and read the scriptures, Jesus wasn't saying, 'Get caught up in the liturgy and rhetoric.' To me he was basic, giving the real, sayin' 'This is what's going on.'"

Despite his exciting stage presence and imposing appearance, the Living Instrument is disarmingly lighthearted and even philosophical about the eviction of the HipHopEMass from Trinity. It doesn't really surprise him. The ceremonies and rituals were always front and center in the Episcopal Church. Even Poppa T made sure the rap services never really deviated from the Book of Common Prayer in structure if not in style.

Speaking for himself, he could take or leave the ceremonies. Sure, they're important to a point, but when dealing with lives he believed it was more important to meet people where they are, to talk real people to real people.

"They say, 'Jesus Jesus!' " D-Cross opines about the end of the HipHopEMass at Trinity. "But he sat down with some of the worst of people, broke bread with them. Let's be real. Religious figures can sometimes get wrapped up in the high and mighty instead of getting down to what it's really about. With Trinity, the young people were turned away because of how they dressed. Jesus said come as you are."

Now the young people from Forest Houses would have to find somewhere else — anywhere else he was afraid — to hear someone speaking to them in their language. He knows as well as anyone that Poppa T made mistakes, and if it had been him he would have done some things differently. But he also knows no one is perfect. It's not easy staying true to one's self and one's God. We all slip and stumble. The original twelve disciples themselves suffered from some control and ego issues, even arguing about the seating arrangement in heaven once Jesus was on his throne.

For a man who can sound like thunder, the ocean, or any musical instrument you can name, D-Cross's Southern accent is particularly bad when impersonating the priest. But D-Cross is kind, and he knows that God doesn't give us gifts in neatly wrapped packages because we're the wrapping, sometimes torn or wrinkled or otherwise imperfect. Hip-hop, to him, is an expression, and even though the HipHopEMass services are institutional and liturgically correct, ultimately it didn't matter.

"With the HipHopEMass I had an opportunity to be an instrument for someone," he says gratefully. "A word I said or sound I made might have been of service to somebody else."

Glory is handsome in his MTA uniform on the Staten Island ferry, where he checks tickets. Jahneen sometimes runs into him there. He seems happy. His daughter, Zion, is talking now, just a few words, but there will soon be enough for a prayer.

He's moved to Washington Heights, and even though it's been quite a while, he has good memories of those weekly HipHopEMass services at Trinity or traveling to a school or a park in the early days, sometimes just him and the priest without the band or even a boombox. They used to attract a gathering of kids by rapping and preaching right there on the spot. He would simply start freestyling from their point of view, as if he were the one hanging out in the park or the projects, waiting and listening for something real.

When he rapped about the Lord, it would just come out. He didn't have to think about it. Rapping is when he felt touched by God. "If you know who the Lord is it's not even hip-hop. It's preaching, it's prayer," he says about his experience.

Because of the HipHopEMass, his life got going in a different direction than he ever thought it would, and he seems proud of the fact that when he turned nineteen he was the first to be baptized through the ministry. "When they threw that water on me," he preaches to kids in the PJs, "it was amazing." The way he grew up, he hadn't seen himself ever getting baptized, so this seemed like a new chance, a new life.

He had asked Poppa T to be his godfather "because we could talk about anything, not just about the music," he explains. "I used to call him about things, questions about the Bible, about when I was troubled, or about getting married. I just felt I could come to him, and he had knowledge. We were like a family in that time. Even the band was like my brothers."

And then the arguments and finger-pointing started. Everyone, it seemed, was ganging up on Poppa T. At first he had no idea Trinity didn't want him and the other hip-hop parishioners there. The attacks on the priest and the HipHopEMass surprised and disturbed him. What about forgiving trespasses, he wondered. After the meeting when he stood up for Poppa T and hip-hop in front of the entire congregation, the HipHopEMass took to the road, and he was busy graduating from high school. He stayed in touch with the priest, but he was no longer part of the regular crew. He was working two jobs and needed to make money. He still rapped God's word, but he was a father now and his daughter's mother would soon be his wife.

He was only twenty, but the HipHopEMass he had joined when he was seventeen seemed distant in so many ways. Being part of it, though, and knowing Poppa T had been a blessing. They both had done so much for him. Knowing that God is love and that hip-hop is beautiful made him feel that he really was acceptable to God after all.

Rap is not what most people think it is — the meeting at Trinity taught him that — but God talked to him that way. Just because he doesn't talk to everybody that way, the young rapper believed, it doesn't mean hip-hop is not of God, but only that it's not for everyone. Glory might not see God by praying as the elders of Trinity did, but he could find him in rap. Yes, the HipHopEMass was a blessing. If nothing else, Poppa T gave him a chance to do what he loved for God, and he believed God put the priest in his life to help him grow in his relationship with him. Maybe it sounded crazy, but that didn't mean it was any less true.

⁓☙⁓

"I wish Poppa T the best," says Sam. "I'm gonna miss him." After a long pause he starts to say something and then interrupts himself. Finally he says again, "I'm gonna miss him."

Sweeping the church steps, he is conscientious about his duties as Trinity's sexton but unsure about his future here. "This church doesn't have a priest," he says. "It's hard to give trust to somebody else. I trusted him. He was honest with me. Sincere. He listened all the time. He was a true friend to me and my children. He was a true friend to Forest Houses and the South Bronx."

Living in the PJs, working at Trinity, Sam is now the most direct link between Trinity Church and Trinity Avenue, and he wonders what he's going to tell the children who ask what happened, who want to know why the HipHopEMass isn't there anymore. He'll just tell them "Poppa T moved on," he decides. No more explanation than that. But he knows it's a real loss for the 'hood and the children not having the rap ministry right next door anymore, showing another way to live and look at their lives. Back in the day, when the plans for Forest Houses were redrawn to save Trinity from demolition, the projects had made room for the church. Now he wasn't so sure the church would make room again anytime soon for the projects.

"A lot of children gonna miss him," he says, sweeping.

Every August Cool Clyde returns to Rosedale Park across from the Bronxdale Projects, the place he calls "the birth park of hip-hop." That's where he used to spin for fun back when no one knew the ultimate reach of what they were doing. Now he's the organizer of Raising Kings and Queens, an all-day hip-hop celebration of the unity, peace, and love that hip-hop's founders and the EMass disciples never stopped preaching. He dares to believe that the ones who weren't there in the beginning might hear hope in the remix, like they all once did back then.

He still can't believe universities teach courses on hip-hop now. "Hip-hop was supposed to be a phase maybe twenty years ago," he says triumphantly. "It was supposed to be around for five years, and that was supposed to be the end of it. But now, to look at it and see it's going in so many different directions, that's a great thing. Today one of the key things is to be able to use hip-hop in the churches for spiritually positive things."

Once again Kurtis, Poppa T, and the HipHopEMass are invited to appear at the Raising Kings and Queens event. He wants people to see the rappers and the priest together, to see white and black, young and old all together. By bringing people together, he wants to send a message, to show them what hip-hop is really all about.

Before becoming one of the earliest DJs for the HipHopEMass or joining Kurtis at the Hip Hop Church in Harlem, Cool Clyde used to think that hip-hop wasn't "the right thing to do" while in church. "Now we can feel comfortable expressing ourselves through hip-hop music and talking about the Lord," he says. "That's something I learned being part of the HipHopEMass."

⤚⥱⤙

"What a great resurrection day!" he beams. "You had two resurrections. You had the resurrection of Jesus Christ and the resurrection of Kurtis Blow. Praise the Lord, redemption! Praise the Lord!"

It was Easter Sunday 2007 when he became a licensed minister. The ceremony, "the first step to becoming ordained," took place at a "Baptist, but more Pentecostal" church in Philadelphia, where he had cofounded another Hip Hop Church America congregation. Five host churches for the national youth ministry now reached from Harlem to Los Angeles. He MCs and preaches at them all whenever possible as well as visiting new cities and sanctuaries to spread the word to the Hip-Hop Nation. It seems as if he is on the road just as often as during his early rap career when he was one of hip-hop's most wanted.

His dream of different kinds of churches joining together to worship God through rap was coming true. "It doesn't matter if you're a Baptist, a Presbyterian, a Calvinist, a Methodist," he takes pains to emphasize. "Pentecostal, Episcopalian, A.M.E. Zion, it doesn't matter. Hip Hop Church is your church."

He also takes pains not to be too proud, not to confuse his growing ministry with his former career. Pride, he says, is a sin. He objects when other hip-hop pioneers include pride along with peace, unity, and hope as hip-hop's original inspiration and purpose. The nature of things has shifted for him, but the transformation is ongoing, he knows. It never ends.

"Paul says in the Bible, 'I die every day,'" he explains. "What that means is every morning when he wakes up he's a new person, he's a new creature in Christ. . . . So when you wake up in the morning, you open your eyes and just thank the Lord for making it possible to take one more breath and try to live more Christ-like. This is our mission; this is our walk."

Ever since he was a little boy, when God found him in his bed in Harlem, his dream was to check out how life really is when you try to live it without sin. He had failed. He had leaned too much on his own understanding, believed too much in the promises of the world. Now he was once again trying to awake to that dream.

He knows he's not alone. He partners with other Christians from any denomination that will have him, and his ministry is alive and growing. Within hip-hop itself, he is grateful the number of rappers, MCs, and DJs living and speaking the Word is also growing. He leans forward excitedly talking about how Grandmaster Kaz got saved. His buddies, "guys who have been out there like myself sinning for thirty, thirty-five years, are coming to Christ, man! Grandmaster Kaz got saved. MC Shane got saved, Master P. This is amazing! God is moving on people."

He points to Reverend Run of Run-DMC, formerly billed as the Son of Kurtis Blow, MC Hammer, Christopher Martin, formerly of Kid 'n' Play, all of them once-successful rappers now focused on inspirational and religious projects. Those who introduced rap to the streets and those who took it out into the world were now helping create not just a service here or a ministry there but an increasingly influential hip-hop church movement. As one of the first rappers to introduce racism and social dislocation into rap's early party with "The Breaks," "Hard Times," and "Tough," he knew what it was to carry a message worth hearing. Now he had one again.

As far as he was concerned, controversies within the hip-hop church movement over whose God was in the remix or what Christian love looks like today could be subsumed in the Holy Spirit. Weren't they all animated by the same desire to know and share the love of Christ?

"My ultimate hope for not only the HipHopEMass but all of the hip-hop ministries — Holy Hip Hop, HipHopEMass, Hip Hop Church, and all of Christian rap — is to bring souls to Christ," the new minister declares.

He is moved to think that now there are children who are part of the first hip-hop generation whose love of rap has more to do with God than the thug life. For them there is the possibility that hip-hop can be redeemed and again represent the unity, peace and love he insists it was always meant to. This is it, he believes, their chance to help create the world Afrika Bambaataa, Cool Clyde, he, and the rest had envisioned. Through the grace of God, they could again see hip-hop as a vision of hope for the future, a refusal to be anything less than alive, and a declaration that the new world was here for the creating. If they could do that, then these children would prove to be the true descendants of hip-hop's pioneers and prophets. For him, they would be a promise fulfilled.

He had it straight now. None of it was in vain. Everything he saw, everything he lived through, what was gained and what was lost, the struggle to understand scripture and stay true to rap, all of it prepared him for this work, for these children. They spoke the same language, and so he could tell them all he knew, everything he had learned the hard way. He could tell them about God.

"This is Minister Kurtis Blow Walker!" is his outgoing message now. Finally, the King of Rap knows his purpose. He has found his *telos.*

❦

On a cold, damp Sunday at the end of February, the priest delivered his final sermon as rector of Trinity Church of Morrisania. "I have learned that evil is real, the devil is real, on these streets but also within the church sometimes, within ourselves." His voice was strong and filled the sanctuary. "These children and teenagers in the towers outside know this evil. This is a reality.

But there is also a greater reality. As Dr. King said, the arc of the universe is long but it inclines toward love."

Once again entering into the season of Lent, coming up on three years since Adam had held the neighborhood hostage, Poppa T hewed to the scripture and order of service being observed throughout the worldwide Anglican Communion. He had chanted the verses of Luke 4:1–13, where Jesus enters the wilderness for forty days and nights and Satan offers him riches, power, everything if only the Son of Man will bow down and worship him.

"The church and those of us in it can be in the wilderness, but that is no excuse to hate or to hurt," he continued. "We can give love because we've been shown love. This is, after all, a church. We're not guarding a museum. We're nourishing the garden of life.

"Jesus' words were to the children, but they have to do with all of us — the children of Israel, of this country, of the South Bronx. The witness of children of the civil rights movement, of the struggle against apartheid, of the HipHopEMass, all show how the children work in a tangible way, how they sacrifice or are sacrificed."

The priest could hear a chorus of amen's as he concluded, speaking from his heart. "It's important as we rebuild and as we live on in this church and in this world not to demonize our brothers and sisters. Stand up against what is wrong, but I pray you don't demonize me, or any person anywhere. Please forgive me for all my sins and let that forgiveness be real."

Afterward at the priest's farewell brunch, Paula went to him, looking beautiful in a stylish fur hat to ward off the chill. At first there were no words.

"I'm sorry," she said finally, sincerely. "I feel so sad."

"Me too," the priest replied.

"I'm sorry things didn't work out."

"Paula, it is working out. God has his plan."

And then they said good-bye. The priest returned to Mr. Warren, Marjorie Jones, Lillas Bogle, and several others who had tried to keep the doors open to the street. The congregation sent him off with a grand Caribbean feast and testimonials from some of the families of those elderly parishioners he had buried over the years.

Seated on a big "bishop's chair," the priest felt as if love, finally, was all around him. He was presented with a purse filled with five-, ten-, and twenty-dollar bills collected from people at the church and in the neighborhood so he would be safe and taken care of on his journey to his new parish.

~≈~

Shortly before he left for Atlantic City, Marjorie Jones, Lillas Bogle, Mr. Warren, and several others from Trinity said their good-byes over lo mein and green tea at the Chinese Buffet in Co-op City. "His family took him to dinner," Mrs. Jones states as a matter-of-fact. "We joked that Mr. Warren and Lillas Bogle were his parents and Jeanie Seaman, Sonia Bird, and I were the sisters and teased him about how he was going to explain having a black family to his new church in Atlantic City."

She admits she was still a little upset. "The animosity with which he was met during his last days at Trinity and how he handled it made many of us say he was truly a man of God. . . . Lots of people did not share Paula's view and can't believe he was forced to resign. A lot of the older people were extremely disturbed when they found out Father Timothy was leaving. They felt he was doing a good job."

Mindful that the core of her faith is "love, compassion, forgiveness, and service," however, Mrs. Jones feels "we have battered and bruised each other enough." While she loves and supports the priest, she is "still a member of Trinity and will continue to be a member of Trinity with all its foibles and warts and shortcomings." She does not want to ostracize or malign anyone. She wants to be part of the healing. Father Timothy may be her brother, but everyone at Trinity — everyone — is part of her church family.

The smile returns to her voice when she shares how one of the oldest members of Trinity, Agatha Lake, ninety-two, whom everyone calls Mother Lake, called the priest her grandson. At the end of the dinner, amid the paper lanterns and Chinese décor, someone pulled out a camera and they took a family portrait.

⎯⦈⦉⎯

Old School Sam, Paradox, and four others from the PJs moved Poppa T one snowy afternoon.

"Ghetto Movers, we get the job done!" Sam yelled to the young men hauling over two hundred boxes full of the priest's belongings, including his library of over three thousand books, down the narrow stairs. Brandon and Kareem, two big guys in the neighborhood who had never stepped foot inside the church but knew Poppa T from the street, showed up to help Sam move the piano down the steps.

"You leavin'?" asked Brandon, a rapper as foul-mouthed as they get. "We can't have that."

"Well, you never came to church," Poppa T scolded. "I could have used your help sooner."

Late that night with the U-Haul truck finally packed and Sam behind the wheel, the priest read one more time a farewell card from one of the teenagers in the traditional congregation. Inside in bold penmanship was written, "The pathway to Atlantic City is the pathway home to the South Bronx."

ASCENSION

Thursday, May 17, 2007

Over three hundred people stream through the front doors of the Historic Church of the Ascension in Atlantic City, the cool salt air blowing from the boardwalk a block away. Poppa T is about to be installed as the twelfth rector of the 128-year-old congregation and eighty-year-old vestryman Buddy Grover couldn't be more excited. With its cracked plaster, rattling pipes, and leaky roof, the old basilica had not seen such a crowd in years, he confides.

"We only get fifty faces total for both Sunday services, but we're hoping to grow with Friday night hip-hop," he says, his eyes bright and smiling.

Many of Ascension's seventy-five official members are in attendance as well as eighteen honored well-wishers from Trinity, led by Lillas Bogle, Marjorie Jones, and Mr. Warren. Poppa T later even joked that the quorum of Trinity's vestry who made the overnight trip were perhaps making sure he really had moved.

Kurtis was still on his way from Selma, Alabama, interrupting a twenty-eight-city tour to attend with rappers Ricky B and Chris Flow of The Trinity. Poppa T himself had not yet arrived by the time the DJ started spinning and the pews began to fill. The Missionary Men, Rock, and Paradox were already in the house, but Jahneen, the only other original HipHopEMass disciple scheduled to appear that night, would not be coming. She was at her home on Staten Island. The symptoms of Hodgkin's disease had recently returned. She lay in bed that night, at peace this time and unafraid.

As the early arrivals made their way past the bronze crucifix beside the front doors, Poppa T was hurrying up Kentucky Street in white Bermuda shorts and black nylon socks pulled to his knees, collar on and vestments flung over his shoulder. Inside the soaring sanctuary, aged ushers in suits handed programs to young men sporting fades or dreadlocks as the priest entered the sacristy through a side door. With smiles and booming Southern hospitality, he greeted the crush of clergy from North Carolina, New Jersey, Delaware, and Alabama, members of the gospel choirs of Ascension and St. Augustine's, old friends, young rappers, and the excited members of Ascension's vestry, all ready and waiting to begin.

Within moments the strong smell of incense filled the basilica as the white-robed host of acolytes, priests, bishops, and choirs gathered for the entrance rite up the center aisle. Suddenly the organist began to play a traditional prelude and as the crowd rose to their feet, the procession moved toward the chancel. With Poppa T stopping at almost every pew to hug and greet friends and parishioners, Reese, a twenty-year-old female Jersey rapper, read the Proclamation of Isaiah over the organ prelude: "Do not remember the former things, or consider the things of old. I am about to do a new thing; now it springs forth, do you not perceive it?"

The crowd was a disconcerting mix of ancient church matriarchs in their Sunday best, surprisingly shy children, young African American men sporting oversized hoodies and jeans, some worn-down men looking for a place to rest, and affluent Southern suburbanites in suits and dresses. Colorful African headdresses on a few women dotted the pews. Two tough looking teenagers in do-rags nodded to ladies in elaborate hats and the women nodded back, alike in dignity. One unshaven man sat quietly at the end of a pew near the back, his weathered face expressionless beneath lank, shoulder-length hair. Whatever he was thinking, whatever he was feeling, his stillness seemed like a turning point, the axis upon which a ministry, a church, a spirit could pivot and rest.

Later, as the Missionary Men rapped "The Gospel," they exhorted the crowd to wave their hands in the air and the first hands that shot up belonged to a young gay priest from the diocese of Delaware and an African American lady in royal purple stooped with age, barely able to raise her hand shoulder high.

After Ascension's deacon chanted the words from the Book of Luke of the resurrected Jesus appearing to the disciples — "Thus is it written, that the Messiah is to suffer and to rise from the dead on the third day, and that repentance and forgiveness of sins is to be proclaimed in his name to all nations" — Poppa T chanted the same verses in Spanish. Several young men got up to leave and Mr. Grover intercepted them near the door and invited them to stay.

"We're Muslims," they explained. "We only came to see Kurtis Blow. We don't want to be disrespectful of the worship."

The elder vestryman assured them there was no disrespect. Kurtis was coming and there was no need to leave. They are welcomed at Ascension. Everyone is welcomed here.

Jim Lemler, the director of mission for the Episcopal Church USA, delivers a brief and lively sermon, quickly warming to the crowd. His words and friendly oratorical style elicit laughter and supportive exclamations of "Amen" and "Word."

"For we are celebrating the new thing that God is doing," Father Lemler says, evoking Reese's reading of Isaiah. "So then, friends, what is this new thing that God is doing here? How is God renewing us, recreating us, lifting us up? These are the questions for us and for this occasion. Just what new thing is God doing in this world, which he loved so much that he gave his only son so that human beings everywhere might live? In this Episcopal Church of ours? In this HipHopEMass movement? In this congregation at a new beginning in it's mission? In this man's life and leadership" — and here he gestures to a beaming Poppa T — "as he embarks on a new part of his journey?"

Father Lemler pauses long enough for a siren to be heard in the distance.

"What new thing is God doing in your heart and in your life?"

He pauses again as if expecting an answer.

"Because God *is* doing a new thing, right here and right now," Father Lemler says in conclusion. "God is shouting to you and to me: 'I am doing a new thing!' Let us join in the shout!"

The crowd bellows back, "I am doing a new thing!"

"And let us praise God who has released us for life."

"Amen!" some say.

"Word!" others say.

And then there is the presentation of the gifts of ministry to the new rector, including rich-looking gold vestments from the new parish that make Poppa T's face flush with pleasure. Ascension's congregation applauds the visitors from Trinity as Mr. Warren steps forward and presents Poppa T with the nearly empty bottle of Cavalier Rum they had shared that day, huddled together in the South Bronx stairwell. It is, he says, the "first holy relic of the HipHopEMass."

Then members of Grace Church in Alabama, the priest's first congregation, present him with an icon of Martin Luther King Jr. Next, representatives of Ascension give him a beach ball and a sand bucket, saying, "Father, this is for you to know we expect you to have fun as well as bring tons of new members into our church."

Finally Tito, proprietor of Alexander's Shoes and "the final word in rap in Atlantic City," gives the priest a Tupac cross T-shirt, declaring him an "official member" of the local hip-hop community.

During the prayer of dedication, surrounded by such of-ferings and tributes, Poppa T's voice breaks. "Oh, Lord my God — " he repeats after a long silence, before continuing in a strong clear voice. "I am not worthy to have you come under my roof; yet you have called your servant to stand in your house and to serve at your altar. To you and to your service I devote myself, body, soul, and spirit. Fill my memory with the record of your mighty works, enlighten my understanding with the light of your Holy Spirit, and may all the desires of my heart and will center in what you would have me do. Make me an instrument of your salvation for the people entrusted to my care, and grant that I may faithfully administer your holy Sacraments, and by my life and teaching set forth your true and living Word. Be always with me in carrying out the duties of my ministry. In prayer, quicken my devotion; in praises, heighten my love and gratitude; in preaching, give me readiness of thought and expression; and grant that, by the clearness and brightness of your holy Word, all the world may be drawn into your blessed kingdom. All this I ask for the sake of your son and savior Jesus Christ. Amen. Word."

Standing behind the priest, the bishop turns to the assembly. "Meet your new rector." As the people applaud, Poppa T keeps turning round and round, red with emotion, taking in his new church, new home, new congregation.

As Ascension's newly installed rector presides over the Eucharist table, Reese and Rock lead the congregation in singing "This Little Light of Mine" and by the second verse the clapping starts. Buddy Grover steps forward and kisses the aged lady in purple slowly making her way to the altar. Together they look at the faces in the pews and smile at what they see.

After communion and the prayer, Poppa T delivers the Pontifical Hip Hop Blessing. After the final exhortation — "Stay up, keep your head up, holler back, and go forth and tell it like it is!" — he adds, hand held high, "Let us make New Jersey new!"

⁓⧫⁓

Marjorie Jones didn't stay for the "Ascension + Hit the Sky07 Concert" following Poppa T's induction and the liturgy of the Holy Eucharist. Truth be told, she never really liked rap. She just wanted to support the young people and Father Timothy in his efforts to keep the church alive. As long as she can go to Trinity's 11:00 a.m. Sunday mass and have her incense and candles and traditions, she is as happy as can be.

She knows they're all getting old, that the church won't live if they don't bring the young people in. If that means a hip-hop mass or a calypso mass or a reggae mass so be it. As long as it's built on the Word of God she's all for it.

Back in the South Bronx, people in the neighborhood stop her on the street now and ask how Trinity could have let the rap ministry go. Well, it looked as if the HipHopEMass would survive. This church in Atlantic City seemed to understand that hip-hop didn't demean them in any way. There was even an old man with a walker who could barely move, but he was participating in everything. From what she saw, there were people inside Ascension from every level of society. She didn't see the upper crust cringing or the hip-hop youth turned away. No, she thought the installation was beautiful, proving that there's room at God's table for everybody.

As long as the newcomers remember they are in a church, she welcomes them to come and praise God in any form they wish. But now that the rap was starting in earnest, she would take her Feast of the Ascension back to the EconoLodge.

⌒≋⌒

Heads are bobbing to Reese's rhymes, and when she steps off, the Missionary Men jump in with "Father, I Will Lean." The elders have pretty much cleared out except for Mr. Grover and other vestry members, but curious African American and white teens and twenty-somethings filter into the pews. Among them, one young man dressed in black who had been sitting in the back row all night has moved up front, and the bishop is now seated at the end of the fourth row.

Kurtis and The Trinity arrived from Alabama in the midst of Poppa T's installation, and when Jahdiel and Monk lay down their mikes, he runs out front, star power at full wattage.

There were those at New Shiloh Baptist Church, the largest congregation in Atlantic City, who asked Kurtis to cancel his HipHopEMass appearance at the Historic Church of the Ascension, Poppa T later found out, but he was here now and the crowd's excitement fills the old basilica.

Decked out in trademark white, "Hip Hop Church" emblazoned on his T-shirt, he enters with some high-energy stepping alongside Ricky B and Flow. As they stomp across Ascension's plywood-patched floors, it's as if their intricate steps could blister the already-peeling paint and shatter even more panels of stained glass. Rapping, "I'm Tired of All This!" he has both sides of the center aisle on their feet and caught up in an old-school call and response battle:

"Are ya hot?"

"Are ya cold?"

Tonight Kurtis is clearly hot. This is a concert, not a service, and the showmanship and skills that made him the King of Rap in 1980, that filled arenas and helped bridge the hip-hop underground to the nation, are in full force. He's giving everything he's got to this small crowd in a crumbling church, and the absolute joy Poppa T saw on his face that very first time inside Trinity is back. It suffuses everything he does, every rhyme and step, and everyone there.

Well, almost everyone. A middle-aged African American man asks no one in particular, "Can you understand this?" He's pleasant enough but clearly puzzled. "Okay, g'night," he finally says, turning toward the doors.

But this is what the rest of the crowd came for, and as Kurtis breaks a sweat he shouts, "Anyone out there love Jesus? Throw your hands in the air for the Lord!"

At the first beats of "The Breaks," the crowd seems to surge forward, and when Kurtis asks, "Any breakdancers in the house?" Desmond Staley, eighteen, attending his first Christian hip-hop concert, starts breaking in front of the altar. Airbrushed on the back of his gray hoodie are the words "RIP Roel," a tribute to a friend dead at seventeen.

Poppa T stands in the back by himself, taking it all in. He has put away his new gold vestments and is back in Bermuda shorts, black kneesocks, and loafers. Around his neck are two crosses, his first piece of street bling that DJ Old School Sam had given him, and the latest, an enormous cross with scrolling red lights that read "Jesus Rocks" presented to him by some children here in New Jersey. A nondenominational pastor comes by to congratulate him, remarking, "In thirty-nine years in Atlantic City, I never saw so many young men in a church. Thank you, Poppa T, for teaching us you can't judge a pastor by his Bermuda shorts."

After Kurtis preaches about the love of Jesus Christ, he and The Trinity break into "Just Do It," the last rap of the night. The sound carries into the cool, salty night air, and outside lights glimmer, but they aren't stars, just the electric glow of the nearby casinos.

EPILOGUE

Sunday, May 20, 2007

It is a cold morning and inside Trinity Church of Morrisania the aged members of the tiny congregation wear their winter coats as if preparing to take a journey. There are nine parishioners gathered for the 8:00 a.m. service, only two seemingly under seventy, including Paula. She has returned to Trinity with her mother. They sit together behind Joe Barrett, Mrs. Roberts in a black quilted coat and Paula in a multicolored wrap.

This is the last time the "8:00 a.m. family" will worship together like this. Starting the following week there will no longer be two services at Trinity but only one 10:00 a.m. mass, an attempt to fill the pews and bring the fragments of the remaining congregation together. There are no children, no hip-hop prayer cards, no one from the multitude living in the towering PJs outside. There is not even organ music.

"Father Roberts used to say, 'There is no death,' " a member of the vestry remarks. "Life goes on. The spirit is here. Father Roberts's wife is here, his daughter is here and — I don't say this to put butter on you — the Trinity spirit is here."

A middle-aged priest, filling in temporarily, delivers a brief sermon about heaven. "Heaven is real," he says. "We enter heaven not on merit but on faith." He finishes speaking but does not say what heaven is or how it is made.

The service is liturgically correct. Everything is as it was. Yet nothing seems the same. The spirit that remains here may be tired but it does not rest. That life force could, if wanted, rebuild a church just as once, so many years ago, it remade the borough of fire.

After the supply priest recites the Nicene Creed the people stand and take turns reading aloud from page 386 in the Book of Common Prayer. "I ask your prayers for the poor, the sick, the hungry, the oppressed, and those in prison," Joe Barrett begins, his voice filling the cold sanctuary. "Pray for those in any need or trouble."

When it is Paula's turn she reads, "I ask your prayers for all who seek God, or a deeper knowledge of him. Pray that they may find and be found by him."

"I ask your prayers for the departed," Mrs. Roberts reads next. "Pray for those who have died."

When all the prayers are said and the people are finished, Mr. Barrett leads them in singing "This Little Light of Mine," the same hymn the crowd sang at the Historic Church of the Ascension just a few days earlier at Poppa T's installation. Then they gather in a ragged circle, hold hands, and recite the Lord's Prayer.

ACKNOWLEDGMENTS

For open doors, soft beds, comfy sofas, and warm hospitality during the research and travel for this project, I thank Paul Gauger, Kevin Adams, Ian Holloway, and Patrick Pacheco. In particular, during the gestation and writing of this project, Rachel Hyman, my friend and agent Fred Morris, and David Fikse and John Barrentine opened their homes to me in country and city for much longer than the acceptable three-day visit. The friendship of all my hosts counted more in the writing of this book than even I knew.

Encouragement and support came from many, including Professor Ronald Thiemann at Harvard Divinity School; Bruce Shenitz, who as executive editor of *OUT* magazine championed my feature story on Poppa T for his magazine; and Jamaica Kincaid, who helped at just the right moment.

I also want to express my keen appreciation to Robert Flynt for generously offering his artistry along with his friendship, Tom O'Leary for his eagle eye, Austin Young for making me look good, and Kevin Delaney for sharing DVD interviews from his own film project. To Lucas Smith I offer my heartfelt gratitude and respect. More than an astute editor, he proved himself to be a steadfast ally and a writer's best friend. It couldn't have been easy but he went to the mat when it mattered and I will not forget it.

Jeff Chang's monumental hip-hop overview, "Can't Stop, Won't Stop," provided valuable history and context, as did the Bronx African American History Project directed by Mark Naison at Fordham University. Not only am I am profoundly indebted to Rev. Howard Blunt, former interim rector at Trinity Church of Morrisania, for his significant research on the history of Trinity and his valiant spirit of diplomacy, but also for being a friend to this project and opening doors that would have otherwise remained closed.

I was honored by the stories, ideas, laughter, tears, insights, and contributions of those in the HipHopEMass crew — the rappers, beatboxers, musicians, MCs, and DJs themselves — all those too numerous to name who generously spoke to me from the heart and off the cuff. To Rev. Timothy Holder and Paula Roberts, in particular, I say thank you and, again, thank you. I hope I honored your trust and the short stretch of road we traveled together by telling it as I saw it.

This book would never have been attempted if not for the lifetime of love and the occasional hard truth from my parents, Norma Jean and Vernon Holyoke. I know now that they, along with the rest of my family, have made all the difference. They are my greatest blessing.

Finally, to the young people from the projects of the South Bronx to the shady streets of Chapel Hill who shared what the HipHopEMass experience meant to them, I offer my heartfelt thanks for the invitation into your lives and your world. I especially want to thank the young people at James River Juvenile Detention Center. Our time in the gymnasium and afterward convinced me that this was a story worth telling. Your words and your lives inspired me. This book is for you.